CW00386392

BUCKLAND ABBEY

Devon

THE NATIONAL TRUST

Chapter One has been written by Mary Mauchline; Chapter
Two by Duff Hart-Davis. To both the National Trust is very
grateful. Chapters Three, Four and Five are by Hugh Meller, the
Trust's Historic Buildings Representative for Devon. Equally
important has been the contribution of staff from Plymouth
Museum. The Museum's archive on Buckland and its history is
unrivalled, and much of the information on the abbey and the
exhibits from its collection now on show has been provided from
this source. The Museum has also generously allowed the
reproduction of many of the illustrations contained in this
guidebook.

Buckland Abbey is
presented in association
with the City of
Plymouth Museums and
Art Gallery.

CITY OF PLYMOUTH
MUSEUMS
& ART GALLERY

Photographs: British Library pages 8, 10, 11; National Maritime
Museum, Greenwich pages 22, 30, 31 (left); National Portrait Gallery
pages 21, 28; NT/Nick Carter pages 1, 7, 33, 57; NT/Chris Chapman
page 40; NT/George Wright front cover, pages 4, 13 (top and bottom),
14, 15, 17, 24, 25 (top), 35, 41, 42 (top and bottom), 43, 45, 46, 47, 49, 52, 53,
56, 58, 59 (top and bottom), 61; NT/Mike Williams page 6; Plymouth
Museums and Art Gallery pages 25 (bottom), 26, 27, 29, 31 (right), 38, 50,
back cover; Portsmouth City Museums page 20; Robert Chapman pages
12, 39, 51; Royal Albert Memorial Museum, Exeter page 9; Tate Gallery
page 55; Westcountry Studies Library page 36.

First published in Great Britain in 1991 by the National Trust
Copyright © 1991 The National Trust
ISBN 0 7078 0114 1
Designed by James Shurmer
Phototypeset in Monotype Lasercomp Bembo series 270
by Southern Positives and Negatives (SPAN), Lingfield, Surrey
Colour reproduction by Acculith 76, Barnet, Hertfordshire
Printed in Italy by Amilcare Pizzi s.p.a. for
The National Trust, 36 Queen Anne's Gate, London SW1H 9AS
Registered charity no. 205846

CONTENTS

INTRODUCTION

Despite its remote setting on the western fringe of Devon, Buckland has had an eventful history, which reflects the eminence of those associated with the abbey during the last 700 years.

It was established as a monastic foundation in 1278, the last of 76 medieval Cistercian abbeys to be built in England and Wales. The founder was Amicia, widowed Countess of Devon and a lady of impeccable aristocratic antecedents who also endowed Buckland with vast estates. The cavernous Great Barn, built to store the harvest those acres produced, still exists as a potent witness to Cistercian fecundity.

For over 250 years the monks prospered, occasionally squabbling with neighbours or petitioning the crown when their interests seemed threatened. However, the ascetic Cistercian rule gradually relaxed and the attraction of their way of life waned. At the Dissolution of the Monasteries in 1539, only the abbot and twelve monks remained to be exiled from the abbey.

Within two years Henry VIII had sold Buckland to Sir Richard Grenville, a soldier from a long-established north Devon family, and he, with his son Roger, began converting the abbey into a comfortable house. In 1545 Roger was drowned whilst commanding the warship *Mary Rose*, when she capsized off Portsmouth, leaving a son, another Richard Grenville, to inherit Buckland. He completed the conversion, marking the occasion with the date 1576 in the plasterwork of the Great Hall.

Richard was an ambitious soldier with designs for colonising the New World, but he never secured royal patronage for his schemes. Royal favour was, however, bestowed on Sir Francis Drake, who between 1577 and 1580 became the first Englishman

to circumnavigate the globe. Disillusioned, Grenville sold the abbey, but achieved immortality in 1591 when his ship, the *Revenge*, was overwhelmed in a heroic stand against a Spanish fleet. Drake meanwhile had acquired Buckland and for the next 370 years descendants of the Drake family retained possession – save for a brief period during the Civil War when the Parliamentary Drakes were ousted by their old rivals, the Royalist Grenvilles.

Gradually Buckland was modified to suit the family's changing needs. At the turn of the eighteenth century it was remodelled by the architect Samuel Pepys Cockerell and the agricultural buildings were modernised by the pioneer agronomist William Marshall for Lord Heathfield of Gibraltar, a Drake descendant through the female line who, like so many other owners of Buckland, died childless.

A nephew, Sir Thomas Trayton-Fuller, inherited, but during much of the nineteenth century Buckland was rented out. In 1870 it passed to Sir Thomas's nephew, Sir Francis Fuller-Eliott-Drake, whose wife published an informative history of the heirs of Sir Francis Drake. Their daughter, who became the wife of Lord Seaton, lived on at Buckland until 1937, during which time she restored the Chapel. A year later disaster struck when the abbey caught fire. It was restored, not entirely sympathetically, during the war years and sold in 1946 to a local landowner, Captain Rodd, who presented the property to the National Trust.

Since 1951 Buckland has been administered by the Trust with the City of Plymouth, which uses the abbey to display part of its collections. In 1987 the abbey, exhibitions and visitor facilities were refurbished as part of the 400th anniversary celebrations commemorating the defeat of the Spanish Armada, in which Sir Francis Drake had played such an important part.

(Opposite) A detail of one of the shield-bearing satyrs that support the ceiling of Sir Richard Grenville's Great Hall

THE CISTERCIAN FOUNDATION

The Cistercian Abbey of St Mary and St Benedict at Buckland in south Devon was founded in 1278. It lies on the edge of Dartmoor, hidden deep in the wooded valley of the River Tavy, beside a small and unnamed tributary stream. The Cistercians were very sensitive to the beauty of their surroundings, and the site has all the peace and seclusion associated with the ruins of monasteries of this Order, such as Fountains Abbey in Yorkshire. However, there were always practical reasons for their choice of site – the availability of running water, timber for construction and good building stone in the locality. Buckland offered the immediate isolation 'far from the haunts of men', as decreed by the Order, and the natural advantages essential for a Cistercian settlement.

Buckland was a late and very well-endowed foundation, owning from the outset 20,000 acres besides a large outlying estate in east Devon. The community had, therefore, no experience of the poverty and hardships that beset the early Cistercian houses in England and characterised the beginnings of the Order itself. It originated in France in 1098, when a group of monks retired to the marshy desolation of Cîteaux in Burgundy, from which the Order took its name. Their aim was to renew their

Fountains Abbey in Yorkshire was one of the earliest Cistercian settlements in Britain, founded in 1132

monastic vocation by living according to the basic principles of the early sixth-century Rule of St Benedict, the founder of the Benedictine Order. The fervour and self-denial with which they silently followed the Benedictine pattern of worship, prayer and meditation, and the emphasis they placed on the manual work it enjoined, became the hallmarks of the Cistercian Order they founded. Extreme asceticism threatened their survival, but the compelling example of sheer holiness and the sense of spiritual adventure generated by the movement attracted recruits in this era of the Crusades. They welcomed the challenge of absolute poverty: on the altar were a cross of painted wood and an iron candlestick, the meagre diet contained neither meat nor grease, and underwear and combs were forbidden luxuries. St Bernard, abbot of Clairvaux from 1115 to 1153, was the driving force behind the rapid expansion of the Order. In 1128, the 'White Monks', so-called because their habits were made of undyed sheep's wool, established the first Cistercian house in England at Waverley in Surrey. Early in the next decade, Tintern in Gwent and Rievaulx and Fountains in Yorkshire were founded. Between 1135 and 1154, during the years of civil war in the reign of Stephen, over forty more came into being.

The Cistercians were warmly received in England by Henry I as a civilising force, pioneers in monastic reform and agricultural practice, eager to settle in remote districts and ready to farm any tracts of poor or uncultivated land donated to them. Unsuitable sites, inadequate endowments and natural disasters drove some of the first generation of Cistercian communities almost to ruin, but they survived to become a major influence in the religious and economic life of medieval England. Buckland remained, however, one of the more obscure houses of an Order which developed, in effect, into a multinational corporation. It represents the final phase of the Cistercian colonisation of England, the last of the Devon foundations and the most westerly in the country.

Buckland's founder was Amicia de Redvers, the widow of Baldwin de Redvers, 7th Earl of Devon and Lord of the Isle of Wight. His direct family line became extinct with the death by poisoning of their son in 1262, and her decision to found a Cistercian

The carved stone head above the visitors' entrance door is said to be a likeness of Amicia de Redvers, the founder of Buckland Abbey

abbey situated among the de Redvers possessions in Devon was therefore an act of pious remembrance as well as religious patronage. Amicia's daughter, Isabella de Fortibus, already a powerful landowner in her own right as the widow of the Earl of Albemarle, inherited the family estates and granted her mother land in Devon for the new monastery. In her charter of 1273, Amicia specified those who would be remembered there – Edward I, his predecessor, Henry III, their wives and children, and Amicia's late husband, his family and her own. She added comprehensively all her ancestors and descendants. Monks came from the Cistercian abbey of Quarr on the Isle of Wight at Amicia's request, to pray for the 'health of their souls' and to establish Buckland.

The strength of the Cistercian Order lay in its organisation as a close-knit family of abbeys; each new foundation was in the care of the 'mother' house from which it had been colonised, and was visited annually by the 'father' abbot. Although four Cistercian monasteries already existed in

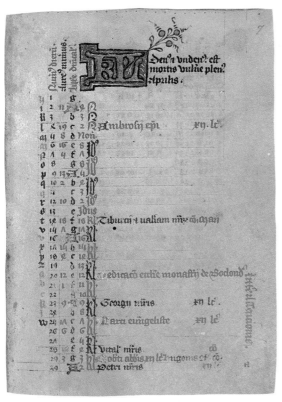

A page from the early fourteenth-century 'Buckland Book', in which the abbots of Buckland's mother house, Quarr Abbey, recorded their advice to the monks of Buckland (British Library)

Devon – Buckfast, Forde (now in Dorset), Dunkeswell and Newenham – Amicia chose Quarr as the mother house of Buckland, for it had been founded by her husband's ancestor, another Baldwin de Redvers, 2nd Earl of Devon, in 1132 as an abbey of the French Order of Savigny, which united with the Cistercian Order in 1147.

The 'Buckland Book', an early fourteenth-century manuscript volume now in the British Library, may well have been used by abbots of Quarr on their visitations to give fatherly counsel and, if necessary, censure. An abbot on his three-day visitation would inquire into the spiritual health of his daughter house, asking about such matters as the observation of silence, and assess the material prosperity of the monastery. At the end, he would request the monks to remember in their prayers

their brethren of Quarr. A list of feasts ordained by the Chapter General at Citeaux is included, giving the day of the foundation of Buckland as 20 April.

By the time that Buckland was established, idealism had collided with reality. Much of the primitive austerity of the early Cistercians had been abandoned and regulations relaxed. Withdrawal from the world had proved impossible and the fame of the Order now rested on economic success rather than on religious zeal. Yet its unity and stability were maintained, a tribute to the vision and ability of St Stephen Harding of Dorset, Abbot of Citeaux between 1109 and 1113. Cistercian monks were required to observe the same customs, follow the same liturgy and occupy monastic buildings laid out, with some exceptions, on the same plan. There was a measure of local autonomy and by the later thirteenth century the authority of the Chapter General had weakened, but the essential structure remained firm.

The site of Buckland Abbey is ancient. An Iron Age earthwork lies to the east of the cloister area and the name Buckland has an Old English derivation, 'book-land', written in a book of Crown leases. When the first abbot, Robert, and his seven monks came from Quarr in 1278, they found a landscape where the main features of Devon were already marked out: high banks, deep lanes and enclosures, some right up to the limit of the cultivable area of the uplands. Towns, parishes, manors and roads are named in Buckland's charters in contrast to earlier monastic charters which may give only natural features, such as trees, stones and ditches, to indicate boundaries.

The rivers Tavy and Walkham formed the western and northern limits, and a third river, the Plym, marked part of the eastern boundary as it flowed south to Plymouth. The stream that finds its way past the abbey down to Lopwell Quay on the Tavy served as the southern boundary. In this settled, populated countryside, Amicia gave the monks the manors of nearby Buckland (known therefore as Buckland Monachorum), Bickleigh, Walkhampton and the more distant, but valuable, Cullompton in east Devon. With these manors came their inhabitants, freemen, villeins and serfs and their families and goods. Moreover, the grants included mills, fisheries, woods, moorland and all the rights and privileges of a manor.

Amicia added the income of the churches of these manors, a device known as 'appropriation of churches', whereby the abbey took the tithe, or tenth part, of the produce of the parish due to the rector for its own use, in this case mainly corn crops. The abbey was then responsible for the appointment of a vicar to care for the parish, who would receive the remaining 'lesser' or small tithes. The Chapter General frowned on this practice, but it was reluctantly accepted, especially if a house could plead dire poverty.

The most significant grant to Buckland in feudal terms was the Hundred of Roborough, which gave the abbot secular jurisdiction over this old English division of land for administrative and judicial purposes. He thereby had to recognise the king as his feudal overlord, a difficult matter to resolve when the Cistercian Order had the privilege of being responsible only to the Pope and to no other authority. In 1279, the year after the founding of the abbey, Edward I's Statute of Mortmain compelled donors of land to religious houses to apply for a royal licence, an act designed to curb the alienation of vast tracts of England which the king could never recover from these institutions. The abbots of Buckland retained their rights in the Hundred of Roborough, but the boom in the monastic acquisition of land was over. Buckland added little to its original endowment beyond two houses in Exeter and Saltash. Amicia had been generous and had acted only just in time to avoid the provisions of Edward I's legislation.

There is all too little information concerning the management of Buckland's estates. The economic prosperity of the Cistercians owed much to their use of lay brothers, and by integrating them into the life and work of the community the Order made a notable contribution to medieval society. The purpose of a lay brotherhood was to free the 'choir monks' (the term used to differentiate them from the lay brothers) from the more mundane tasks associated with a monastery, but this reserve of unpaid labour tempted the monks to assemble widespread estates. These were consolidated into

A detail from a late fifteenth-century map of Dartmoor, showing Buckland Abbey (Royal Albert Memorial Museum, Exeter)

gaudebunt campi ꝉ omnia que in eis sunt

Harvesting: a detail from the early fourteenth-century Luttrell Psalter, which provides an unrivalled picture of medieval agricultural life (British Library). The wealth of Buckland depended on careful husbandry of its fertile estates

specialised units, known as granges, usually for sheep farming, but also for arable or cattle farming.

Two circumstances made it difficult for Buckland to establish the traditional Cistercian pattern of estate management. Firstly, the abbey knew the system of a lay brotherhood only when decay was setting in. By the late thirteenth century it was becoming much less easy to recruit suitable lay brothers; they were drawn from the locality, usually illiterate and often a liability – rebellious, disloyal and too fond of beer. In 1274, while negotiations for the founding of Buckland were in progress, the Chapter General allowed houses with a dearth of lay brothers to employ hired servants in the monastic kitchen. (Hired labour had been permitted from the first, but never before within the cloister.) Secondly, the structure of established, manorial agriculture inherited by Buckland in 1278 did not lend itself to the creation of the ranch type of farming characteristic of Cistercian granges. Nevertheless, there is evidence, both documentary and archaeological, for the presence of lay brothers at Buckland and for estates farmed as granges.

The fourteenth century was critical for most Cistercian abbeys. Poor harvests, wars against France and Scotland, the Black Death and the consequent economic and social disturbance, and the shortage of lay brothers dictated a complete change of policy. In 1335, the Chapter General finally permitted houses with overstretched resources to lease granges for rent to outside tenants; the monks therefore ceased to be involved in their management and the lay brotherhood withered away. Successive outbreaks of the Black Death ravaged Devon from 1348 and the 'poverty of the abbey' is referred to in 1356. But recovery in the county as a whole was quick, and records of the leasing out of granges seem a feature of Buckland's estate administration only in the next century, for instance Walkhampton from 1486. Certainly by the abbacy of Thomas Olyver (1461–1508) Buckland, like other houses of the Order, was no longer concerned with any direct interest in farming its properties, beyond keeping 'in hand' a home grange for immediate monastic needs.

The Cistercians had a genius for sheep farming and wool production. Buckland missed the peak period of this prosperity in the first half of the thirteenth century when the Order's wool exports made an important contribution to the national economy. However, wool was certainly produced

Penned sheep, from the Luttrell Psalter. The Cistercians were renowned sheep-farmers

at Buckland. In 1347, when Edward III demanded financial aid from the greater monasteries in his war against France, the wool crop of Buckland was so valuable that the abbey ranked second in the list of Devon houses to be approached. Oats was the staple crop, rye was grown, rough pasture abounded for livestock, cattle could be pastured free on the fringes of the royal forest of Dartmoor and cloth had been woven from the rough wool of the native Devon sheep 'time out of mind' in Roborough, according to a fifteenth-century petition to Parliament. A document of 1356 lists among the other produce of the area, flax, poultry, calves, lambs, geese, doves, piglings, milk, cheese, butter, honey and wax, hay, apples and vegetables.

Devon had rich deposits of silver and tin. The silver mines were worked intensively by Edward I from the late thirteenth century, and a 1511 lease mentions a stamping mill on the Buckland estates used to stamp blocks of tin with their owner's mark. It is not clear how important silver and tin were to the Buckland economy, but the wealth of the Cistercian Order in England depended on husbandry rather than on industrial concerns. The abbey did suffer, however, from the use or abuse of

its hospitality by visiting royal officials and the 'poor house of our Lady of Buckland' was sometimes hard pressed. Miners trespassed on the abbey's property and by 1303, the third abbot of Buckland, Geoffrey, was forced to petition Edward I about timber taken from his woods by miners to fuel their furnaces.

In view of Buckland's late arrival on the Cistercian scene and its extensive endowments, it is all the more surprising that the architecture of the abbey marks a return to the austerity and simplicity of the first foundations of the twelfth century which embodied the ideals of the Order in three-dimensional terms. In accordance with Cistercian requirements, Amicia would have had to provide temporary buildings to await the monks' arrival; an oratory, refectory and dormitory were necessary from the outset, 'so that the monks may immediately serve God and live together in religious discipline'. The Buckland community was never large. Only seven monks came with Abbot Robert from Quarr, instead of the apostolic number of twelve normally sent out to colonise a new settlement. (The 37 monks who appeared with him later in a court case would have included lay brothers.) In 1539, twelve monks left the abbey at its dissolution.

The construction of an abbey church was begun as soon as possible. It is an impressive unity, all of one build of the late thirteenth century with no later extension. The cruciform building is small, set 27 degrees north of east, with four bays in the nave and two in the chancel. There were no aisles or triforium, and, as abbeys of the Cistercian Order were dedicated to the Virgin Mary, a separate Lady Chapel was not a feature of their churches.

Traditionally the church of an abbey was set upon the highest part of the site. At Buckland, by contrast, it lies tucked into the steep slope of the Tavy valley below the uplands of Roborough Common, possibly terraced into the hillside. The stone is a slate, known locally as shillet, which has been used for all the abbey buildings, and is found in quarries close to the church. The dressings are of local Roborough granite, a soft type of granite which weathers like limestone. The exterior remains very much in the primitive Cistercian manner, devoid of ornament, a well-proportioned and compact mass of grey stone, totally in harmony with its environment.

The approach to Buckland is from the south, and facing the abbey church the removal of the south transept by Grenville to allow light to enter his Great Hall is immediately obvious. The demolition has left a small courtyard at base level, and the old east wall and part of the west wall of the transept form two sides of this court. Grenville used the east elevation as the outer wall of his new service wing to the right. At the foot of this wall, the two blocked, arcaded entrances to the former transept chapels can be seen. These chapels were a distinctive feature of Cistercian churches. One of the north transept chapels still exists with its thirteenth-century vaulting. The carved head of a woman with outsize ears over the door of the visitors' entrance was probably once a boss in the choir or crossing vaults; it has been suggested that it may represent Amicia. The lower part of the medieval west wall on the left of the courtyard has become the foundation for the outer wall of the projecting structure built to house an early nineteenth-century staircase.

The tower above the crossing appears to dominate the abbey in defiance of the early Cistercian prohibition of towers. In the early sixteenth century, a wealthy abbey like Fountains could afford to

A reconstruction of how Buckland Abbey might have looked shortly after it was built in the late thirteenth century

The south transept of the abbey was demolished by Grenville, but two blocked arcaded entrances to the former transept chapels can still be seen in the west wall of the kitchen wing

raise a fashionable tower in the Perpendicular style, evidence of the change in Cistercian attitudes over four hundred years. In England, however, low Norman towers were often built, and at Buckland the effect of height is due mainly to the removal of the transept roofs. The original roof line of the south transept is clearly visible on the southern face of the tower. Moreover, it is likely that there was a low coping in place of the present battlements, which are not medieval. The crenellations on the north side of the chancel roof belong to the defensive works carried out as a result of Edward III's licence of 1337 to crenellate the 'dwelling-place and church' of Buckland, during the Hundred Years War when the French threatened Plymouth and the surrounding district.

The west front of the church reveals emphatically the almost archaic nature of Buckland's Cistercian architecture, severe and plain. Traces of the original west windows can be made out, single-light openings and simple mouldings of a very restrained pattern, for the early Cistercians believed that colour, carving and ornament distracted the mind from duty and devotion. The west doorway recalls the days of the lay brothers, who used this entrance into the west end of the nave reserved for their worship. They attended fewer services, but the whole community came together for the three great feasts of the Christian year, Christmas, Easter and

Ascension. When the lay brothers were no longer part of the abbey establishment, the first three bays were probably sealed off and the space may have been assigned to domestic use or storage. The floor was lowered to create a cellar during this century and the opportunity for detailed examination thus destroyed. The last bay of the nave and the crossing where the monks sat became Grenville's Great Hall, entered from the north side. It is almost certain that the nave would have been vaulted in wood. The crossing does have springers for a stone vault, but it is questionable whether it was ever built.

During the period of the First World War Lady Seaton discovered behind the screens passage the east end of the monastic church, which had been in use as a servants' hall. With the help of Lord Seaton, she created the present Chapel in 1917 for Roman Catholic worship, using the lower part of the two-bay Cistercian chancel and the medieval fragments found in the excavation of the site. The tiles discovered under the floor are of interest – red,

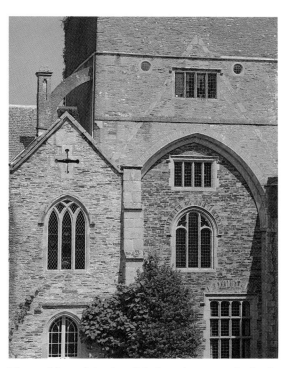

The roof line of the demolished south transept is clearly visible on the southern side of the tower

green and yellow. They are glazed and patterned with various designs, a fish, a dragon and a lion, this last associated with the de Redvers arms. A connection with Plympton, the nearby Augustinian priory, where similar tiles exist, suggests either that one of these two houses was producing tiles or that they shared a common source.

The structure of the church is best appreciated on the top floor, where a long gallery was made after fire destroyed much of the building in 1938. At the east end of this, one stands high up under the crossing, enclosed within the four transverse arches. On them the stability of the entire building depended, and the stone springers of the vault merit inspection. But the most notable feature is the lower east arch, pierced by an opening filled with Decorated tracery of the fourteenth century and rebated for glass. This window at one time overlooked the chancel roof, implying that its roof must have been lower than those of the nave and transepts, yet a further indication that at Buckland are preserved characteristics of the first Cistercian churches.

Traces of the medieval church can be identified throughout the interior. Typical are the late thirteenth- or early fourteenth-century mouldings, akin to those at Netley, the Cistercian abbey in Hampshire; the stone corbels on the first floor, carved with the symbols of two of the Evangelists, the winged ox of St Luke and the eagle of St John; and the circular staircase winding up in the thickness

The delicate tracery of this arch on the top floor once formed an exterior window looking east over the abbey chancel

of the corner of the vanished south transept just inside the visitors' entrance on the left.

The heart of monastic life was here in the abbey church, where the 'opus dei', the work of God was performed in the daily round of worship, the seven offices or services of the Cistercian liturgy. A slow form of Gregorian chant was used and the compiler of the Buckland Book refers to the ignorance and neglect of the old ways too prevalent in monasteries of his Order; his purpose was to revise the musical content of the liturgy and root out any modern accretions. Buckland was in the traditional pattern, both in architecture and liturgy a return to the old purism. The day was divided into worship and work, the latter now interpreted in a much wider sense, but occupying the customary period of four hours morning and afternoon. A third aspect was the 'lectio divina', times of slow, meditative reading to foster spiritual growth. Cistercian abbeys had no schools and only novices were instructed; truth was revealed through spiritual vision, not intellectual attainment. Prayer was the essence of the silent Cistercian vocation.

The family relationship of the Cistercian monasteries was emphasised by the common layout of their cloister buildings, although allowance was made for local conditions. After the construction of the abbey church, the drainage and plumbing were of primary concern. The Cistercians were the finest water engineers of their age. At Buckland the contours of the site and the drainage made it necessary to place the cloister to the north of the abbey, as at Quarr; in most English houses of the Order, it lies to the south. There are no standing buildings in the cloister, although limited excavation has indicated that substantial foundations remain to be uncovered in the future. To envisage the medieval monastic scene at Buckland, one must therefore turn to better preserved Cistercian cloisters such as that at Fountains Abbey, where the Chapter House, refectory, kitchen and lay brothers' range can be clearly identified.

The area of the cloister at Buckland must have been restricted, since the nave of the abbey church was no more than 69 feet in length, and this formed the south side of the cloister. Here, in the shelter of the covered alley that protected monastic cloi-

This stone corbel, carved with the winged ox of St Luke, is typical of the decoration that once enlivened the Cistercian abbey. It is now in the Georgian Dining Room

sters, the monks sat during the periods of the 'lectio divina' and heard the evening reading at Collation, facing north through the stone traceried openings. To their right rose the bulk of the north transept of the church. This formed the north end of the east cloister range, seen in Bucks' engraving of the abbey dated 1734, and demolished probably in the 1800s. A recent survey confirms that the eastern cloister range would indeed have occupied this position. The central room in this range was the Chapter House, where a chapter of the Rule of St Benedict was read every morning to the monks when they assembled for the daily Chapter Meeting to deal with the religious and secular business of the community.

Over this range stretched the monks' dormitory, situated so that they could process in their night boots straight into the north transept and down into the choir at about 2.30am, to keep their Vigils, the first service of the day. Their 'reredorter', or latrine block, would have been situated at the far end of the dormitory. Cistercian planning was a model of convenience and efficiency, for it was important to conserve time and energy in an existence devoted to 'the work of God'.

The location of the northern cloister range is marked by a section of medieval wall, opposite the church. This would have contained the refectory, flanked in this case by the warming house to the east and the kitchen to the west, the latter so placed that the monks' refectory could be served through a hatch on one side and the lay brothers' refectory on the other. The north cloister wall contains blocked windows and doorways which, it has been suggested, might be associated with the fireplace or ovens of the kitchen. Certainly the wall was at one time part of a building, perhaps of several. Excavation carried out in 1984 in the area beyond this section of medieval wall revealed its potential importance as the site of the north cloisters.

The two buildings situated outside the wall, Tower Cottage and the Cider House, which do not belong to the National Trust, are monastic in origin and have been much altered. Tower Cottage may have served as the abbot's house, placed, as in abbeys of this Order, in the more secluded area of the monastery near part of the infirmary, where the Buckland community would benefit from a more clinical approach to everything from serious injury to general 'aking'. The building is unlikely to have served as the gatehouse, since it lies so near the cloister and the abbey gatehouse is described in the fifteenth century as being to the west of the monastery. However, most of Buckland's traffic must have passed along the route by Tower Cottage down to the river, for the Tavy was navigable to seagoing vessels of the medieval period as far as Lopwell Quay on the abbey boundary.

The 1984 excavation centred round the Cider House and its garden, confirming within the latter the presence of medieval buildings which almost certainly represent the north-west corner of the cloister. This would in typical Cistercian plan have been associated with accommodation for the use of the lay brothers. Their quarters formed the entire west range of the cloister, giving them direct access to the court outside. This building projected beyond the western elevation of the church to increase its size, as, for instance, at Sawley Abbey in Yorkshire, where the nave of the church is also of four bays only. Their refectory would have been at the other, northern end beside the monastic kitchen, the central bays used for storage, and their dormitory on the floor above, running the length of the range. The reredorter and perhaps their infirmary would probably have been sited in this north-west corner; but how far the abbey took into account its lay brothers is a matter for speculation, considering its late foundation and the imminent demise of the system.

The industrial area of the establishment lay around and behind Tower Cottage and the Cider House, beyond the north cloister wall. There were workshops for the masons, the smiths, the carpenters and the abbey bakehouse and brew-house. Beside the stream were fish-ponds and on the banks quarries and orchards.

The long, two-storey building on the steep slope above the abbey (now the National Trust's shop and restaurant), has also been the subject of recent archaeological and architectural investigation. The findings suggest that the building was constructed as a stable and not as an infirmary or guesthouse and that, at some time in the late monastic period, it was converted to domestic use. Although it may then have become a guesthouse, it is more probable that it was a dwelling for the reeve or farm manager, in charge of the home farm of the monastery. The roof is of great interest, a fifteenth-century structure to judge from the large size of the Roman numerals cut in the timbers to guide the carpenters. The two sections of each jointed cruck, and the original, upper cross-ties are pegged together with wood. Only the post-medieval cross-ties and braces are nailed. The last bays at the east and west ends have been added later and features like the chimneys and fireplaces are also post-medieval. During the last hundred years before the Dissolution of the Monasteries such a building would be well adapted for the needs of a farmer, his cattle and storage, for the wider doorways would have given the access needed by cattle.

The outstanding architectural feature of Buckland is the Great Barn. It was clearly planned for a prosperous community and belongs to the same period as the abbey church, about 1300. It shows the same reliance on mass and proportion to give an impression of strength and endurance. Its dimensions seem to dwarf the church, and it is set obliquely only 80 feet from the chancel. The exterior elevations derive their dignity and rhythm from a progression of buttresses, closely spaced and interspersed with narrow slit windows. The barn has all the characteristics of primitive Cistercian industrial architecture, like the forge at Fontenay in France and the mill at Fountains Abbey. Over the vast, shadowed interior an arch-braced roof of fifteenth-century date was constructed, in contrast to the jointed cruck roof of what is now the shop above the restaurant. The putlog holes where the medieval scaffolding was inserted are still open and dovecotes remain above the great medieval doorways. The barn would have been used for storage, the crops, wool and hides from the abbey's estates gathered in at each end, and a winnowing area in the centre.

The administration of the purely monastic aspect of the abbey's life remained always in the hands of monastic officials, called obedientaries: the prior, who was second-in-command to the abbot, the sacrist, responsible for the ordering of the services as guardian of the church, the precentor, in charge of the music, and others, all with confusing and separate accounts, until in 1307 Edward I ordered the appointment of bursars in central control of monastic finance. The cellarer, however, was the domestic head of the abbey, with widespread authority for the organisation of its estates. By the Tudor period, secularisation had so invaded the monastic world that the administration of these had been given to lay officials. At Buckland, the steward of the abbey, the Marquess of Exeter, was assisted by a staff of sub-stewards, bailiffs and receivers, and the monks, divorced from these material concerns, enjoyed the profits. Henry VIII made the Marquess, his cousin, patron of the abbey. The transfer of power at the Dissolution was all too easy. Within the cloister, too, change was apparent. An example

(Opposite) The Great Barn with its superb fifteenth-century arch-braced roof. It would have been used to store the harvest from the rich Buckland estate

is the indenture between Abbot Thomas Whyte (1511–28) and the organist, Robert Derkeham, whereby the latter was to instruct the boys of the abbey and give any monk who so desired, tuition in music and playing the organ. In return, Derkeham had a salary of £2 13s 4d a year, a furnished room over the west gate, 5 oz of bread and a quart of beer every night, a wax candle from 1 November until 2 February (Candlemas), a gown worth 12 shillings a year and 30 horse loads of faggots for his fire. At the Dissolution, this agreement was honoured.

Abbot Whyte was forced to resign by the Marquess of Exeter in 1528. He went unwillingly, protesting that despite his age he could still carry out all his duties, although he could not ride. He asked that John Toker, known to be of 'untoward conversation', should not succeed him. Nevertheless Toker became abbot in 1528 and set about exploiting his position. He leased the tithes of Buckland Monachorum and other churches of the monastery to his brother, Robert, and his two nephews, and Robert was in addition a well-paid bailiff of Cullompton.

Such malpractices were but one symptom of the malaise affecting religious institutions in general in the early sixteenth century. At his accession in 1509, Henry VIII had seemed the model of an enlightened Renaissance prince, and men like Sir Thomas More and Abbot Huby of Fountains had hoped for the reform of the Church from within the ecclesiastical establishment and the religious foundations. Huby's ambition was to re-establish the primitive Cistercian values through a revival of spiritual discipline and encouragement of university studies, a policy fully in accord with the scholarly and theological character of the Renaissance in Tudor England. But the 'Great Matter of the King's Divorce' drove the Reformation in England into other channels, in which the king's personal, political and financial motives were paramount. Henry was styled 'Head of the Church in England' in 1534 and the abbeys were doomed, less as obsolete outposts of papal power than as the owners of a substantial area of Henry's kingdom and the guardians of accumulated treasures. Buckland survived the fall of the lesser monasteries in 1536 by having an income of over £200 a year, the cut-off point. Its mother house of

Quarr, however, was dissolved and two of the monks came to Buckland. After three years of uncertainty, and even fear, the greater houses 'went down' in a state of voluntary compulsion. In a sweep of dissolution, Buckland surrendered to the royal commissioner William Petre on 28 February 1539; seven other Devon houses were dissolved within the space of eight days.

Abbot Toker was given a pension of £60 per annum and, in 1557, became vicar of Buckland Monachorum; he was there apparently until 1564. His twelve monks received pensions ranging from £5 6s 8d to £3 6s 8d per annum and eight of them were drawing their pensions as late as 1553. The value of Buckland was assessed at £241 17s 9¼d, Tavistock at £902 and Plympton at £912. No inventory of goods appears to survive, but the treasure of a Cistercian house in lead, plate and furnishings was usually worth much less than its estates. Buckland was leased for £23 3s 5d per annum to George Pollard of King's Nympton in north Devon, probably the brother of Sir Hugh Pollard, the west Devon commissioner.

The spoils were divided among the King's supporters. Sir Richard Grenville of Bideford, whose ancestor of the same name had founded in 1130 the Cistercian abbey of Neath in west Glamorgan, wrote to Thomas Cromwell in 1539 that he 'was as glad as any man of the suppression of these orgulous [vain] persons and devourers of God's word . . . takers away of the wealth of this kingdom and spies of the dewffelys [devilish] bishop of Rome'. Two years later he was rewarded for his loyalty by being granted the right to buy Buckland. For £233 3s 4d he got the former church, the monastery buildings, the home farm and 568 acres of land together with the neighbouring woods. With its barns, dovecotes, orchards, gardens and ponds, Buckland was ideally suited to become a gentleman's residence. The two and a half centuries of Cistercian Buckland had come to an end.

CHAPTER TWO
GRENVILLE AND DRAKE

By far the most famous tenants of Buckland Abbey were those mighty Elizabethans, Sir Richard Grenville and Sir Francis Drake, who between them owned the house from 1563 until 1596. The period was one of high opportunity and danger for England: as enmity with Spain smouldered, flared into open war, died down and flared again, Elizabeth I's sea captains were voyaging to the ends of the earth and making momentous discoveries. Yet the history of Buckland during these years was as peaceful as its setting: no battle, no insurrection, no siege, no royal visit, not even a fire disturbed the even tenor of life in this fold of the wooded hills that run down to the River Tavy – and in the absence of dramatic events at Buckland, it is most rewarding to concentrate on the careers of the two celebrated owners.

The paths of their lives crossed and re-crossed in striking fashion. It was Grenville who hoped to lead a grand voyage of exploration to the South Seas in the mid-1570s, but it was Drake who finally got the chance and made the first English circumnavigation of the earth, between 1577 and 1580. It was Grenville from whom – through agents – Drake bought Buckland when he returned from circling the globe. It was Grenville who took the first colonists to Virginia in 1585, and Drake who rescued them a year later – passing Grenville, by then also on a rescue mission, during his voyage home. Above all, it was on board the *Revenge* – Drake's favourite ship, which he had commanded against the Armada – that Grenville fought his last action off the Azores in 1591.

The Grenvilles came from the strip of coast between Bideford and Bude on the borders of Devon and Cornwall, a family of the gentry, established in the area at least since the time of Henry II, perhaps even since the Norman Conquest. Their main home was Stowe, just inside Cornwall in the parish of Kilkhampton, but they also owned a town house on the quay in Bideford (both have now vanished). For generations they had done well, in an unspectacular way; but then, according to the historian A. L. Rowse, a 'new and active strain, of immense and passionate energy', entered the family during the sixteenth century, along with 'a harsh domineering note . . . betraying signs of overstrain and unbalance'.

Until October 1540 Sir Richard Grenville the elder (our man's grandfather) was Marshal of Calais, then England's last outpost overseas. When relieved of his command, he returned to England, and in May 1541 was rewarded for his services to Henry VIII by being granted the right to buy Buckland.

It was an opportune moment, so soon after the Dissolution, for anyone to acquire property; but Sir Richard's particular purpose in buying Buckland was apparently to provide an estate for his son and heir, Roger, then in his early twenties, and he called the place Buckland Grenville. It is clear that Roger lived briefly at Buckland, perhaps in one of the monastic outbuildings, for on 28 August 1544 he buried one son, Charles, at nearby Buckland Monachorum.

Fate frustrated old Sir Richard's plans for his son. On 19 July 1545, as Henry VIII's fleet prepared to attack the invading French off Portsmouth, his flagship, the *Mary Rose*, suddenly heeled over and sank, drowning all but about 40 of the 700 men on board. Among the victims was Roger Grenville, the ship's captain.

So young Richard – born in June 1542 – lost his father at the age of three. His mother married again, and her second husband, Thomas Arundell, settled at Clifton, a few miles down the Tamar from Buckland. There Richard grew up, and the undulating, well-wooded country above Plymouth became more of a home to him than his family's traditional haunts on the north coast 50 miles away.

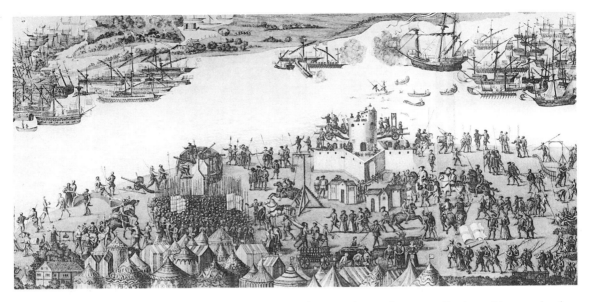

The sinking of Henry VIII's flagship, the 'Mary Rose'. Among the casualties was the captain, Roger Grenville, Sir Richard's father

For a few years Buckland itself passed back to his grandfather, and when *he* died in 1550, he left the place to his wife, Dame Maude, during their grandson's minority. She seems to have had plans for turning the church into a house, for old Sir Richard, in his will, specified that she might fell timber for 'the building of the mansion place'. Within a few months, however, she too expired.

Little is known of Richard's childhood. If he went to school, there is no record of it. More likely he received lessons from a tutor at home. Then, in the autumn of 1559, at the age of seventeen, he went as a student to the Inner Temple in London, which then offered general training in business as well as in law. Not long after his twentieth birthday, on 19 November 1562, the violent streak in his character suddenly erupted when he became involved in a street-fight near St Clement Danes church and ran through Robert Bannester, a London gentleman, with his sword, mortally wounding him – an act for which he may have been briefly gaoled, but for which he was granted a pardon.

On 28 June 1563, soon after he had come of age, he obtained licence to enter his estates. It seems that he was short of money, for he sold some land at Buckland Grenville and Buckland Monachorum to his cousin Nicholas Specott, who had been with him at the affray in London; and he did not tackle the remodelling of the abbey, whose church still stood empty. Instead, he returned to live at Stowe, and late in 1564 or early in 1565 married Mary St Leger, the elder daughter of Sir John St Leger, whose home was at Annery, outside Bideford. This generation of the family, also, was cursed with the high infant mortality common in those days: on 10 December the Grenvilles buried their first son – another Roger – in the churchyard at Kilkhampton.

Next Richard took up the habit of the landed gentry and went off to the wars – in 1566 to Hungary, where he fought under the Emperor Maximilian against the Turks, and three years later to Ireland, where he was appointed Sheriff of Cork and succeeded in putting down a rebellion, but also spent a great deal of money. Again he sold land at Buckland to help finance these expeditions. By early 1570 he was back at Stowe, and a portrait of him painted in 1571 makes him look every inch the adventurer. With his fair hair and blue eyes, he is very much (as Rowse points out) a man of Devon; yet it is not the colour of those eyes, so much as the look in them, that arrests attention four hundred years later. That steely, challenging glance pro-

Sir Richard Grenville in 1571 (National Portrait Gallery; on loan to Montacute House, Somerset)

claims Grenville as a man of action, certainly – but also as one harbouring pent-up aggression, who might easily be moved to sudden violence, a dangerous man to cross.

In April 1571 – the year of the portrait – he was returned to Parliament as Knight for the Shire of Cornwall, and thereafter was often in London. Gradually, however, his main interest shifted from land to sea, from martial to maritime adventures, and in the early 1570s he devoted much time and effort to planning a voyage of exploration in the Pacific and beyond.

Geographical knowledge, in Elizabethan times, was still intoxicatingly vague: the gaps in it were so huge that they fired men of imagination and courage with immortal longings. Passionate argument raged about the disposition of the earth's continents. In 1519–20 an expedition led by Ferdinand Magellan had become the first to sail round the world, but no English sea captain had managed to emulate his feat. By 1569 the leading cartographers Mercator and Ortelius agreed that America was an island; but who knew what fabulous lands might lie undiscovered in the vast expanse of the South Seas? Some men believed that America was separated from Asia only by the Strait of Anian, and that this channel offered the best route to the riches of Cathay; others held that a ship sailing up the east coast of America, and on past Labrador, would come eventually to the North-West Passage, and so to China that way. Either route, if it could be established, would give English sea captains control of far eastern trade without their having to round the Cape of Good Hope.

Fascinated by the challenge and the opportunity, Grenville formed a group of adventurers. Most came from his own family circle, but they included William Hawkins, a merchant of wide experience, and by then the leading citizen of Plymouth. Between them the group could boast four good ships, which cost £5,000 in all; Grenville and Hawkins jointly bought the largest, the *Castle of Comfort*, a powerfully armed private warship of 240 tons. Their hope was that the Queen would take a share in the voyage – which she sometimes did, whether covertly or in the open – and in 1573 Grenville petitioned her to sanction the enterprise.

Queen Elizabeth I, who frustrated Grenville's scheme to sail to the South Seas by her indecision (National Maritime Museum)

His first proposal was for a combination of exploration and empire-building: that the fleet should explore the South Seas 'for discovery of sundry rich and unknown lands, fatally (and, it seemeth, by God's providence) reserved for England, and for the honour of your Majesty'. The patent he sought was 'to discover lands, territories, islands, dominions, peoples and places unknown . . . and specially such as have the Pole Antartic elevate, and the dominions of the great prince commonly called the great Cham of Cathay'.

The project was presented to the Queen and her Lord Admiral on 22 March 1574, and for a while Grenville thought that royal sanction would be forthcoming. Preparations went ahead. By May his fleet was ready to sail, and the Spanish, getting wind of his plans, denounced him as 'a great pirate'. By June he actually had permission, but the Queen made it contingent on him first giving help to the Earl of Essex, who was beset by difficulties in

The Kitchen was built by Grenville as part of his conversion of Buckland from a Cistercian abbey to a private home

Ireland. Grenville helped raise a force to fight across the water – and later was commended for rendering such prompt assistance; but by the time the danger in Ireland had subsided, the summer – and the season for sailing – had gone.

Grenville's frustration is easily imagined; and now a sudden change in the political atmosphere conspired to dash his hopes. All through her reign the Queen had been notoriously fickle in her attitude to Spain, vacillating between defiance and co-operation as each course seemed, in turn, the more expedient. In August 1574, after a period of tension, the Convention of Bristol set a new basis for better relations between the two countries; after it the Queen could scarcely sanction an armed expedition into the South Seas, over which Spain claimed a monopoly. So Grenville's licence was withdrawn at the last moment. With Queen and the Council in a mood to humour Spain, geographical enthusiasm focussed for the moment on the possibilities of the North-West Passage, and the tough Yorkshireman Martin Frobisher gained official approval for a voyage to that quarter, setting out in February 1575 on the first of three courageous attempts to find a way through the frozen seas beyond Labrador.

Grenville, though bitterly disappointed, did not give up. While Frobisher was away on his first expedition, he presented a discourse to Lord Burghley, the Lord Chancellor (whose portrait hangs in the Great Hall), in which he again pressed the claims of an alternative route to Cathay, proposing that he should sail through the Strait of Magellan 'and so ascend from the equinoctial along the western course of that Atlantical island' – that is, up the west coast of the two Americas – until he found the elusive Strait of Anian in the far north. Again, however, his plan failed to find favour, and he finally gave up his grand design.

No doubt it was his plans for a deep-sea voyage that drew him back to live near Plymouth once more. Some time in the early or mid-1570s he at last addressed himself to the task of converting Buckland Abbey into an agreeable home. His scheme for so doing was unusual. He did demolish many of the old domestic buildings and the cloisters; but instead of leaving the abbey to stand as the village church or

go to ruin, and building a new house nearby, as most men did when they acquired monastic property, he converted the church into a dwelling by dividing up the nave into a great hall with screens passage and two floors of chambers above. He kept the square tower and most of the church's outline intact, but removed the south transept, to let in more light, and built a new service wing with a large kitchen where the visitors' entrance now is, and added a staircase extension. The Grenville arms on the label stops of a window in the building now known as the Guesthouse show that he altered that too, although what he did with it is no longer clear.

The result of his labours was a solid and comfortable house, rather than a grand one. The building which emerged was certainly unusual, but neither beautiful nor particularly distinguished. Its one grand room, the elegant Great Hall, is modest in comparison with the splendid interiors of contemporary houses such as Burghley in Lincolnshire, yet it contains one feature of compelling interest. Over the fireplace is a plaster frieze showing the figures of Justice, Temperance, Prudence and Fortitude, and above them the date 1576, which suggests that most if not all of the rebuilding must have been finished by then. But it is the fine plaster frieze on the west wall that deserves attention. In this strange composition a soldier has turned his war-horse loose and sits under a vine, on which he has hung up his shield. Skulls peep from inside the trunks of trees.

Does all this signify that Grenville, at the age of 34, had retired from wars and maritime adventure, to live the life of a country gentleman? Given his character and later achievements, that seems impossible. Is the frieze then ironic, the wry comment of a man deeply frustrated by the failure of his attempt to sail the southern ocean and make himself a national figure? Either way, it is a disturbing composition.

Whatever Grenville's feelings, he settled for the next four years at Buckland, and from that base conducted much business in the West Country, often as a representative of Government. In 1577, for instance, as Sheriff and head of the judiciary, he moved against the well-known Catholic recusant Francis Tregian of Golden, near Truro, who had been harbouring a priest, Cuthbert Mayne. Gren-

The plaster frieze on the west wall of the Great Hall may symbolise Grenville's retirement from the sea to the quieter life of rural Buckland, or frustration at his lack of achievement

ville himself led the raid on Tregian's house and took the priest into custody – with the result that Mayne was hung and quartered at Launceston on 30 November, his head being set on a post there, and his quarters on posts at Bodmin, Tregony, Barnstaple and Wadebridge. In the zeal with which Grenville carried out this order from the Council, one can detect at least a powerful sense of duty, perhaps even a touch of officiousness and bloody-mindedness, as if he poured into relatively minor local tasks the energy which he would have liked to expend on larger designs; and it is clear that the Government found him a most efficient agent. For his many services he was knighted in October 1577.

Why he left Buckland so soon after completing its reconstruction, we shall probably never know. The reason may have been purely financial: the age was one of inflation, and Grenville perhaps ran short of funds, especially after lending money to his hard-up, hard-drinking in-laws, the St Legers (in return for his taking over their debts, they granted him the fee-simple of the island of Lundy, off the Devon coast). Perhaps, as he reached middle age, he simply wanted to return to Stowe, his family's ancestral home. It may be that he did not much like Buckland anyway. In any event, at the end of 1580 he sold – or, strictly speaking, mortgaged – the abbey to two agents acting on behalf of that master mariner, Francis Drake.

Drake had been born, in about 1545, on a farm at Crowndale, a hamlet on the Tavy only 3 miles north of Buckland, and no distance from Clifton, where Grenville grew up. Yet his background was entirely different. Far from being members of the landed gentry, his family were of yeoman stock, and his father Edmund was a lay-preacher who taught his eleven children at home, largely from the Bible. In 1549, when Francis was only four or five, the family were caught up in the violent riots which greeted the New Prayer Book. They sought sanctuary first in Plymouth, then in Kent, where they lived on a hulk in the Thames, and Francis went early to sea on a coaster plying in the Channel. Yet although ships and the sea became his life, he remained at heart a West Countryman, and returned to Plymouth or its immediate environs whenever he could. When, at the height of his fame, he chose for his coat of arms the motto *Sic Parvis Magna* – great achievements from small beginnings – the words accurately reflected his rise in the world.

In person he was stockily built, with round head and reddish beard, a cheerful manner, and the ability to talk straight to anybody, from the Queen down. Enemies called him an arrogant upstart – and no doubt he was; but he was also immensely courageous and energetic, an inspired and inspiring

A miniature of Francis Drake as a young man (Drake Gallery; on loan from Plymouth Museums and Art Gallery)

commander of men. At a critical point in his voyage round the world he himself proclaimed to his crews, 'I must have the gentlemen to haul and draw with the mariners, and the mariners with the gentlemen' – and his ability to make all ranks pull together was one of his greatest strengths as a seafarer.

Among the motives that drove him to mighty deeds, three overriding forces stand out: his burning Protestant faith, his intense patriotism, and his hatred of Spain. This last was ignited by an incident

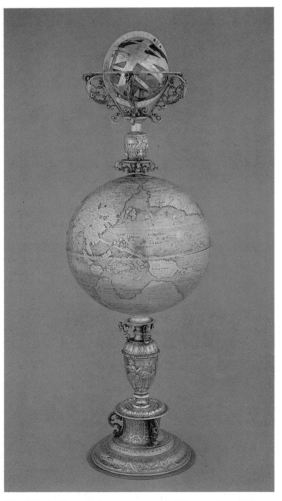

The Drake Cup. It is engraved with Mercator's world map of 1587 and may have been given by Drake to his friend, Sir Anthony Rous of Halton, Cornwall (Drake Gallery; on loan from Plymouth Museums and Art Gallery)

on the coast of Mexico in 1568, when, on his first voyage across the Atlantic, Drake had sailed with his cousin John Hawkins of Plymouth, collecting slaves from the coast of Africa and selling them in the West Indies. All went well until they reached San Juan d'Ulua, the centre of Spanish trade and communications, where the Spaniards tricked and ambushed them; Drake escaped, but was separated from the other ships of the flotilla and returned to Plymouth alone, determined to exact vengeance on Spain.

This he proceeded to do, on every possible occasion, for the rest of his life. Three times in the early 1570s he made successful expeditions to the Spanish Main; on the last, in 1572–3, he captured the town of Nombre de Dios, attacked the treasure trains bringing silver and gold from Peru to the coast, escaped with 300,000 pesos' worth of gold, and returned to England a rich man. Yet of his many marauding voyages, none caused the Spaniards greater chagrin and alarm than his circumnavigation of the globe, achieved between 1577 and 1580.

The professed aim of his voyage was closely similar to that of the scheme proposed by Grenville only four years earlier: to explore the South Seas, seek new lands in Terra Australis, then make for the Moluccas and return home via the Strait of Anian. The great difference was that the Queen, who before had denied Grenville permission to sail, now not merely sanctioned Drake's departure, but herself invested in the venture.

Grenville has often been portrayed as a jealous rival of Drake, embittered by his failure to bring off what the other man achieved. There is, however, no evidence to support this view. Drake gained the Queen's backing simply because the fickle political climate had again changed, and whereas a few years earlier Elizabeth had been anxious to pacify King Philip, now she wished to do him active injury, and secretly gave Drake sanction to attack Spanish treasure ships on the coast of Peru.

Drake sailed in July 1577 on board the *Pelican*, with four other ships and a total company of 164 men; and by the time he returned to Plymouth in September 1580, he had passed through the Strait of Magellan, sailed up the coast of Peru, ballasted his ship with Spanish silver and gold, landed on the shore of California, crossed the Pacific, reached the East Indies and the Spice Islands, and returned via the Cape of Good Hope, the first English sea captain to encircle the globe.

His achievement, consolidating his earlier reputation, made him by a long way the most famous private citizen in the world. Yet so nervous was he when he returned that he did not dare come ashore until he knew how the political land lay; instead, he anchored in the lee of St Nicholas Island, off Plymouth, until his wife and the Mayor came out to meet him. His worries were unnecessary. The Queen summoned him to London, welcomed him in triumph, and, by knighting him on board his own ship (renamed *The Golden Hind*) at Deptford next April, gave open defiance to the King of Spain. So vast was his booty that it was reckoned enough to meet the cost of an entire year's government; most of it was taken under heavy escort to London, but the Queen privately told him to keep £10,000 for himself, and the same for his crew.

While Drake's pockets were burning with Spanish gold, Grenville had again run short of money. So within two months of his return Drake had agreed to pay the very large sum of £3,400 for Buckland Abbey, its contents, and 500 acres of land.

Because Drake did the deal through two intermediaries, John Hele of Plymouth and Christopher Harris of Plymstock, historians believed for years that he tricked Grenville into selling him the estate. Now modern scholarship has revealed the error of this notion: expert analysis of eight contemporary documents shows that Drake's two representatives took Buckland over on a strange form of mortgage, which gave them the right to hand the place back to Grenville, and to recover their money, if they so decided, in March 1584. In other words, at the end of 1580 Drake *lent* Grenville £3,400; the loan allowed him to inhabit Buckland, and also gave him the unusual right of choosing, after three years, whether to keep the property or hand it back in return for repayment. The implications of the transaction are clear: Grenville urgently needed cash, and Drake was equally keen to invest some of his spoils in property.

Messrs Hele and Harris acted as Drake's attorneys, but he himself must have been directly involved. He surely went, for instance, to inspect the abbey, and so see whether or not he approved of Grenville's conversion. It is not clear when he actually moved in: perhaps in August 1581, when he gave up the lease of a house which he had been renting in Plymouth; perhaps when he took formal possession of the abbey, in November 1582. The second date seems more likely, for on 17 September 1581 he became Mayor of Plymouth, and during the year of his office had many duties in the town.

His eagerness to convert bullion into property is strikingly borne out by another recent discovery: that in October 1582 he invested a further £1,500 in buying no fewer than forty freehold properties in Plymouth, as well as some leasehold interests in the Plymouth Town Mills, and leases in other property besides. Suddenly he became one of Plymouth's leading landlords, and it is disappointing that, in spite of various claims, nobody is certain which house he himself used when he stayed in town. At much the same time he increased his property in the county: in 1582 the Queen gave him the manor of Sherford, near Plympton, and later that year he bought the manor of Yarcombe, in east Devon. Later still he acquired the manor of Sampford Spiney, some 5 miles north east of Buckland.

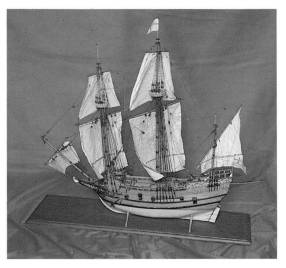

A model of 'The Golden Hind', the ship in which Drake sailed around the world (Drake Gallery; on loan from Plymouth Museums and Art Gallery)

Francis Drake in the early 1580s, at the height of his fame (National Portrait Gallery; on loan to Montacute House, Somerset)

Once established at Buckland, he travelled frequently back and forth between there and Plymouth – most often on horseback, sometimes by river. His importance in local affairs stands out from the records surviving in the Widey Court Book, which show how messengers were frequently despatched to him, or ran errands on his behalf: 'Payment to Sir John Humphreys for carriage of letters to Sir Francis Drake ... Sending Sir Francis Drake's warrant to Plympton ... £5 for a supper for Drake and his lady and other justices ... Item paid Peter Vosper to go to Buckland to know whether the judges did come.'

Somehow it is hard to imagine this short, square man at ease in his large, square country house. No doubt he entertained handsomely, but one has the impression that terrestrial surroundings meant little to him. His true home was the captain's cabin high on the poop of a ship. Certainly in the fourteen years during which he owned Buckland he made practically no mark upon its fabric: apart from some oak panelling, which may possibly date from his time, there is hardly a trace of him – except for a few prized possessions – in the building. It was Grenville, not Drake, who made Buckland what it is.

There is also a certain melancholy in the fact that no children were born to Drake or grew up here. His first wife, Mary Newman, died childless in 1582/3 after thirteen years of marriage; and his second, Elizabeth Sydenham, a beautiful and well-born young woman whom he married about two years later, also failed to produce any offspring. For much of the time, especially when Drake was away at sea, the house must have been empty and echoing.

Just as on the north coast the Grenville family did much to build up the trade and stature of Bideford, so in the south Drake contributed handsomely to the development of Plymouth, promoting the port's trade, improving its defences, and above all directing the construction of a new water supply in the form of a leat, or aqueduct, which ran from the headwaters of the River Meavy at Burrator right into the town.

Local affairs thus kept him tolerably well occupied while he lived at Buckland, yet during his tenure of the abbey he by no means rested from travel. Whenever the Queen needed his services, or would sanction a foray, he sallied forth – to maraud in the Spanish Main in 1585–6, to singe the beard of the King of Spain with his audacious raid on Cadiz in 1587, to play a key role in the Armada campaign a year later, to launch a second (but this time disastrous) raid on Cadiz in 1589, and finally to sail on his last voyage in 1595. For all these grand endeavours, Buckland was his springboard.

During these years Drake's affairs seemed to entwine curiously with those of Sir Richard Grenville. In the mid-1580s Grenville was much occupied with the task of strengthening Cornwall's coastal defences: the curving jetty in Boscastle harbour was rebuilt by him in 1584. But he was also drawn by his cousin Walter Ralegh into projects for planting an English colony in the New World, and in April 1585 he left Plymouth with a fleet of seven ships which deposited 107 men on Roanoke Island, off the coast of Virginia. A year later, knowing that the colonists would need reinforcement and re-supply, Grenville set out again, this time from Bideford – only to find the party gone. And who should have come to their rescue? Drake, who chanced to be passing on his way home, found them in distress and took them off.

Both men fought prominently in the campaign against the Armada – Drake as Vice-Admiral of the English fleet in his flagship, the *Revenge*, Grenville as commander of a flotilla detailed by Queen and Council to ferry troops to Waterford and then to guard the western approaches against any attempt by Philip's ships to attack Ireland. Again fate seemed to deal Grenville a poor hand: while he played an efficient but largely negative role in the west, Drake won further renown by capturing the richly laden *Nuestra Señora del Rosario* and her commander, Don Pedro de Valdés, and by harassing the Armada all

Elizabeth Sydenham, painted in 1585, at about the time of her marriage to Drake (Drake Gallery; on loan from Plymouth Museums and Art Gallery)

down the Channel, until the Spanish fleet was dispersed by fireboat attack off Calais and driven headlong up the North Sea.

Grenville, after further service in Ireland, where he struggled to plant English families as colonists in Munster, at last achieved immortality by the manner of his death, in 1591. By then he was a ship's captain of repute: when at sea, he dined, like Drake, off silver plate, to the sound of music, and was said – when he was in his cups – to crunch up glasses in his teeth until his mouth poured blood. No doubt the stories were exaggerated, but they pointed accurately to his wild temper.

In 1591 he sailed as second-in-command to Lord Thomas Howard, who took a squadron of the Queen's ships, reinforced by private men-of-war, to intercept the returning Spanish treasure fleet off the Azores. Grenville's own command was the *Revenge* – considered by many an unlucky ship, from her habit of running aground and springing leaks.

Off Flores Howard got wind of the approach of a large and powerful Spanish battle fleet, and ordered his squadron to stand out to sea. For whatever

The Armada: the engagement of the English and Spanish fleets between Portland Bill and the Isle of Wight on 2–3 August 1588; engraving by Pine (National Maritime Museum). Drake and Grenville both played a prominent part in the battle

reason – whether because half his men were ashore sick, whether because he thought the sails approaching were those of the treasure fleet, or simply because of his own obstinacy – Grenville failed to obey the order, was cut off, surrounded, grappled and boarded by the Spaniards. The crew of the crippled *Revenge* fought off their attackers all day and all night; with astonishing courage and pride Grenville refused to surrender until, fatally wounded, he was carried aboard the enemy flagship, where he died a few days later.

The battle has passed into legend as one of the most heroic actions ever fought, immortalised not least by the haunting imagery of Tennyson's poem, and the stricken commander's final words:

I have fought for Queen and Faith like a valiant
    man and true;
I have only done my duty as a man is bound to do:
With a joyful spirit I Sir Richard Grenville die!

The legend is splendid, but critical examination suggests that Grenville's behaviour was not entirely rational. His contemporary William Monson thought that the loss of the *Revenge* was caused by his violent temper and 'wilful rashness', and among modern historians Dr Rowse has drawn attention to the manic attitude, amounting almost to a death-wish, which brought him and so many fellow countrymen to a bloody end.

Drake's demise was less glorious. A portrait painted in 1590 shows how much he had aged: his hair had receded, his cheeks and eye-sockets had become hollow, his whole face had sunk. By his late forties even the greatest of Elizabethans had become an old man.

His last expedition to the Caribbean, which sailed from Plymouth in August 1595, seems to have been doomed from the start. His name had lost none of its magic. Men flocked to join him, and a large force was assembled: 27 ships manned by 1,500 sailors, and carrying 1,000 soldiers under Sir Thomas

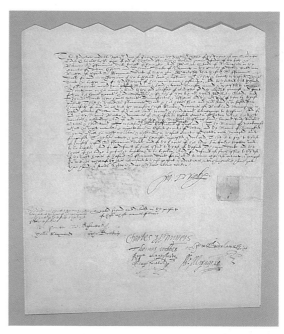

Drake's last will and testament. As he lay dying in the Caribbean, Drake was thinking of Devon: this document lists his property at Buckland and his other estates

Baskerville. Yet Drake's fellow-commander, Sir John Hawkins, now 63, fell ill during the outward voyage and died just as the fleet sighted San Juan. Then, after unsatisfactory and inconclusive manoeuvres on the coast, Drake himself fell victim to the dysentery which was sweeping through his crews. On 27 January 1596, aboard the *Defiance*, aware that his life was ebbing, he signed his last testament in a shaky hand, leaving his property in England to his younger brother Thomas. As he lay *in extremis*, he was clearly thinking of home, for the document listed his possessions at Buckland, Yarcombe, Sherford and Sampford Spiney.

Next morning, 28 January, Drake died, not much over 50 and was buried in a thunder of gunfire within sight of Puerto Bello. 'His body being put into a Coffin of Lead was let down into the sea', recorded a contemporary, 'the Trumpets in doleful manner echoing out their Lamentations for so great a loss and all the Cannons in the Fleet were discharged according to the Custom of all Sea Funeral Obsequies.'

Francis Drake in 1590. In his late forties he was already an old man. Portrait by Marcus Gheeraerts the Younger (National Maritime Museum)

THE DRAKE FAMILY INHERITANCE

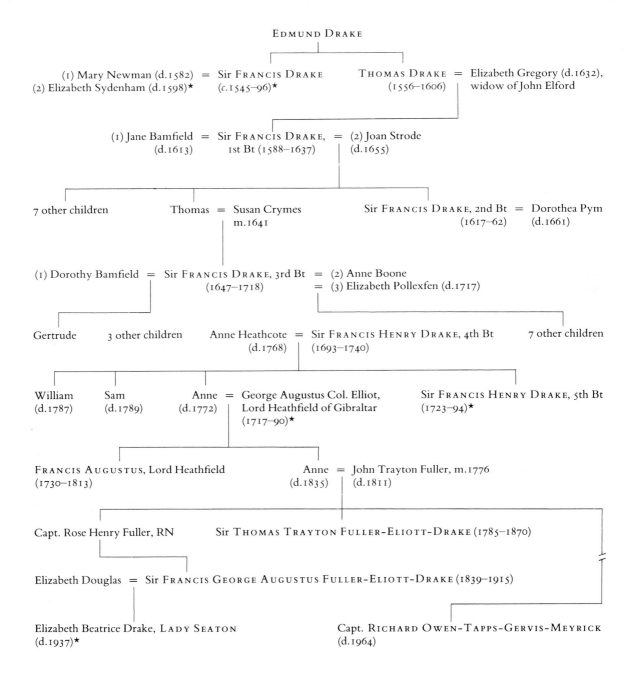

EDMUND DRAKE

(1) Mary Newman (d.1582) = Sir FRANCIS DRAKE   THOMAS DRAKE = Elizabeth Gregory (d.1632),
(2) Elizabeth Sydenham (d.1598)★   (c.1545–96)★   (1556–1606)   widow of John Elford

(1) Jane Bamfield = Sir FRANCIS DRAKE, = (2) Joan Strode
(d.1613)   1st Bt (1588–1637)   (d.1655)

7 other children   Thomas = Susan Crymes   Sir FRANCIS DRAKE, 2nd Bt = Dorothea Pym
       m.1641   (1617–62)   (d.1661)

(1) Dorothy Bamfield = Sir FRANCIS DRAKE, 3rd Bt = (2) Anne Boone
      (1647–1718) = (3) Elizabeth Pollexfen (d.1717)

Gertrude   3 other children   Anne Heathcote = Sir FRANCIS HENRY DRAKE, 4th Bt   7 other children
         (d.1768)   (1693–1740)

William   Sam   Anne = George Augustus Col. Elliot,   Sir FRANCIS HENRY DRAKE, 5th Bt
(d.1787)   (d.1789)   (d.1772)   Lord Heathfield of Gibraltar   (1723–94)★
                   (1717–90)★

FRANCIS AUGUSTUS, Lord Heathfield   Anne = John Trayton Fuller, m.1776
(1730–1813)   (d.1835)   (d.1811)

Capt. Rose Henry Fuller, RN   Sir THOMAS TRAYTON FULLER-ELIOTT-DRAKE (1785–1870)

Elizabeth Douglas = Sir FRANCIS GEORGE AUGUSTUS FULLER-ELIOTT-DRAKE (1839–1915)

Elizabeth Beatrice Drake, LADY SEATON   Capt. RICHARD OWEN-TAPPS-GERVIS-MEYRICK
(d.1937)★   (d.1964)

★Asterisk denotes portrait or sculpture in the house

CHAPTER THREE

DRAKE'S HEIRS

Although none of Sir Francis Drake's heirs ever achieved his national renown, their story over five generations has been meticulously recorded by Elizabeth, Lady Drake, in two volumes published in 1911. She begins with Thomas Drake, the youngest brother and executor of Sir Francis, who succeeded to the estate in 1597 following the death of Sir Francis's widow. Thomas was a sailor like his brother who had accompanied him around the world, but on retirement to Buckland he pursued a new career as plaintiff in 'perpetual law suits' against members of his family, neighbours and Sir Francis's debtors. He won most of the actions, but not all were concluded by the time of his death in 1606. His son and heir was Francis (1588–1637), an Oxford student who, typically for the Drakes, enjoyed an active role in the local community. He became MP for Plympton and later Bere Alston. In 1633 he was appointed High Sheriff of Devon and his support for Charles I was rewarded by a baronetcy. Family matters also concerned him. The estate was extended by the purchase of property at Launceston, Werrington, Yarcombe and Knightshayne and he enhanced his uncle's reputation by publishing *Sir Francis Drake Revived*, and an account of the circumnavigation in *The World Encompassed*, both books providing important source material on the great man.

At the time of Sir Francis's death in 1637, aged 49, Parliament had been dissolved for eight years and opposition to Charles I was increasing among Parliamentarians, whose leaders included three friends of the Drake family: John Pym, John Hampden and William Strode, father-in-law to Sir Francis. The 2nd baronet (1617–62), son of the first and another Sir Francis, had served as a mercenary on the Continent before returning home to marry Dorothea, John Pym's daughter. It was a rash move, for the West Country was overwhelmingly Royalist, including the Grenvilles. After a brief Parliamentary success at the Battle of Modbury near Plymouth, in which Sir Francis took part, fortunes were reversed and Richard 'Skellum' Grenville, the King's general in the west, was rewarded for his military conquests by being granted the estates of three Parliamentary leaders: the Earl of Bedford, Lord Robartes of Lanhydrock and Sir Francis Drake.

'Skellum' (slang for scoundrel) determined to

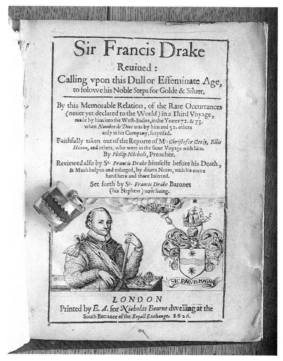

'Sir Francis Drake Revived', published in 1626 by his nephew and namesake to keep alive Drake's memory. On it is the Drake 'Lodestone', a magnetic stone used in compasses and said to have belonged to Drake (Drake Gallery; on loan from Plymouth Museums and Art Gallery)

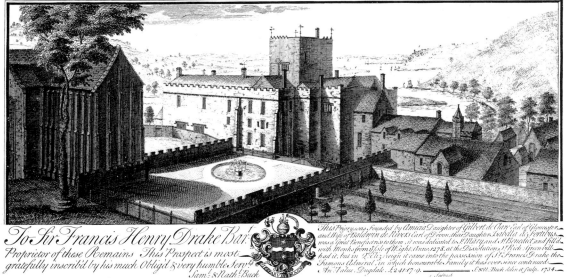

THE EAST VIEW OF BUCKLAND PRIORY, IN THE COUNTY OF DEVON.

The Buck engraving of Buckland Abbey in 1734 shows that the house had changed little since Tudor times

exploit the irony that restored his grandfather's house to the family and he made Buckland Abbey his headquarters whilst he waged a reign of terror on the countryside and besieged Plymouth. Sir Francis escaped with his regiment, the Plym Horse, which he himself had raised, and continued the campaign at the Battle of Langport in 1645 and, under General Fairfax, in the parliamentary advance westward. On 12 January 1646 the general's New Model Army recaptured Buckland and 100 prisoners after a fierce struggle. 'Skellum' had by then retreated to Cornwall and eventually to France, leaving Sir Francis master of his house once more. Fortunately the abbey did not suffer badly during the occupation. Grenville in fact had built a new riding school in the grounds, but Sir Francis and Lady Drake had suffered from being deprived of their estates and their income, and were forced to petition Parliament for pensions.

At the Restoration the Buckland estate comprised 277 acres plus four cider orchards, two gardens, woods, hop yards, nurseries and a small mill. In the abbey itself, Sir Francis is remembered by his coat of arms dated 1655, modelled in plaster above the

fireplace in what is now the Four Lives Gallery. It appears he was a cultivated man as his library included several Italian classics besides novels and French romances. In 1661 he was pardoned by Charles II for his activities during the Civil War and he celebrated the occasion by purchasing a dinner service for the abbey. A year later, aged only 44, he died childless and was buried in the parish church.

The 3rd baronet (1647–1718), a nephew, was once again named Francis and was described as having 'a lively genial temperament'. At the age of eighteen he eloped with his cousin, who died young, and he married twice more, amassing thirteen children in the process. He had trained as a lawyer and took an active part in Plymouth affairs as the town's Recorder, but it was as an MP that his legal training proved most useful in that litigious age. In 1679 he supported the Exclusion Bill in favour of the Protestant Succession, thus provoking the Duke of York, the future James II, to bring an action for damages against him in the sum of £100,000. As a precaution against confiscation he conveyed Buckland to friends and relatives until the danger passed. An inventory of the house contents survives and lists a great deal of silver and pewter, 2 feather beds, 20 tables and cupboards, 48 chairs and stools and 5 tapestries. Less serious, but more wearisome, was a chancery action the baronet waged with his neighbours, the Slannings, over fishing rights on the River Tavy. Proceedings began in 1703, but final judgement and damages were not awarded until 1750 in favour of the Drakes, long after Sir Francis died in 1718.

Little is known about the 4th baronet, Sir Francis Henry Drake (1693–1740), described as 'a popular country gentleman'. He continued the family tradition in taking part in local politics, but otherwise lived an unremarkable life. In 1734 Buckland was engraved by Samuel and Nathaniel Buck, the first accurate view of the abbey, still in Tudor guise, bounded to the east by formal gardens and to the north by a cluster of gabled outbuildings. But this ordered prospect, and Buckland's destiny was already threatened, because in 1732 Sir Francis had inherited Nutwell Court, Exmouth, in Devon, once the property of his brother-in-law, Henry Pollexfen. As a result, on Sir Francis's death in 1740 his son, yet another Sir Francis, chose to spend more time at Nutwell than Buckland, which a contemporary described: 'this decayed place is a sinker and there is absolutely no forethought in the management', adding 'it rains into all the rooms of the house', culminating in the collapse of the Dining Room ceiling in 1754.

The 5th baronet (1723–94) was a stuffy bachelor bibliophile who preferred life at Court, first with the humourless George II, a personal friend, and then George III, following his appointment as Master of the Household in 1771. Perhaps he also avoided Buckland because his mother, the dowager Lady Drake, retained a life interest in the house and allowed a daughter-in-law, wife of Francis's brother Samuel (a distinguished sailor who became a Lord of the Admiralty and Baronet), to use it. Sir Francis's letters suggest he suffered from both melancholia and hypochondria and he took a dim view of his sister-in-law's attempt to brighten up the old abbey, until in 1768 his mother died and he began to make some improvements. During the 1770s the east wing was modernised by fitting out newly panelled rooms reached by climbing an elegant new staircase, prohibited to dogs by the addition of gates, and the Dining Room was improved with a pine dado. The family seat was once again secured until 1794 when Sir Francis died, childless, like his two brothers who predeceased him. He was the last direct male heir to the Elizabethan hero, and at this inauspicious turning point Elizabeth, Lady Drake, ended her book on the history of the family.

A visitor to Buckland at the end of the eighteenth century was William Marshall, the agricultural reformer, who was researching his book *A Rural Economy of the West of England*. West Devon, he considered, was the most benighted agricultural district in England, with Buckland no exception: 'the situation is naturally recluse, and is now rendered truly so, by long neglect'. Fortunately for Buckland Sir Francis's sister, Anne, had married George Eliott, son of the dashing Lord Heathfield who had attained fame and fortune by securing

The dog-gate was installed during the modernisation of the east wing of Buckland in 1770. It was designed to keep dogs off the new staircase

Gibraltar against a Spanish siege between 1779 and 1783. Their son, Francis Augustus, had also followed a military career, obtaining the rank of general, and he succeeded both to his father's peerage and his mother's Buckland inheritance.

With characteristic Heathfield energy, Francis Augustus set about restoring Buckland with the help of his architect, Samuel Pepys Cockerell. Cockerell (1753–1827) had a large London practice and now enjoys a reputation for his whimsically oriental-styled Gloucestershire houses of Daylesford and Sezincote. He also remodelled Nutwell Court into an 'exquisitely precise and austere neo-classical mansion'. At Buckland, however, he was restricted, 'to fit up this House merely for an occasional residence', but he was sufficiently aware of its architectural antiquity to write to Lord Heathfield, 'at all Events no alteration must be attempted to the character of the Building'. The same letter makes numerous suggestions for improving the accommodation, but only one recommendation is known for certain to have been carried out – a new staircase at the south-west end of the

Great Hall, since rebuilt. A great deal more was undoubtedly done, for, in a second letter from Cockerell to Heathfield dated about 1801, he remarks, 'I find this place in very high order and beauty' before explaining his ideas for decorating some of the principal rooms, and his account to Heathfield at the same period for 'designing and superintending the works at Buckland Abbey' amounts to over £7,000.

William Marshall also worked for Lord Heathfield, not always in harmony with Cockerell, who complained in a letter to his employer, 'I am persuaded that the Agricultural arrangements (as well of the Buildings as the Farming) cannot be better done than by Mr Marshall; but he must excuse me for doubting his knowledge of domestic arrangements of another Character and his taste in decoration'. Despite this criticism, Marshall remained popular with Lord Heathfield who bequeathed him £450 on his death in 1813, and the extent of Marshall's influence is demonstrated by the surviving farm journals of 1795–1805 which provide a dour summary of endless labour in the

A drawing of the Guesthouse and Great Barn around 1800, when the agricultural reformer William Marshall was suggesting improvements to the Buckland estate

A view of Buckland in 1832

fields and barns, six days per week, throughout the year by men, women and children. On average about 20 farm workers, 12 oxen and 6 horses toiled at Buckland with the men earning up to 9 shillings per week. Crops included wheat, barley, oats, turnips, potatoes, cabbages, peas, dairy produce, honey and cider. There are separate accounts with specialist tradesmen like the mason, wheelwright, blacksmith, miller, cooper, harness maker, quarry-man and Mr Grear, the mole catcher who caught an astonishing eight dozen moles in October 1800.

Lord Heathfield died childless 'having pass'd a life of general utility', and Buckland was inherited by his nephew, Sir Thomas Trayton Fuller (1785–1870), a soldier who had fought under Sir John Moore in the Peninsular campaign. He assumed the additional family names of Eliott-Drake and in 1821 was created a baronet, but on retirement to Devon he chose to live mainly at Nutwell Court rather than Buckland which was advertised to let on 20 July 1815: 'The house is well furnished and fit for

immediate reception of a family of distinction'. It comprised 3 sitting rooms, 7 best bed chambers, 5 dressing rooms, servants' rooms and offices, stabling for 12 horses and 3 coach-houses. Nineteenth-century tenants included Vice-Admiral Sir Robert Stopford, a Napoleonic war veteran, Sir John St Clair, also a naval officer, and in 1850 Thomas Gill, a Mayor of Plymouth and subsequently the town's MP.

Sir Thomas died in 1870 and once again Buckland passed to a nephew, Sir Francis George Augustus Fuller-Eliott-Drake (1839–1915). In 1861 he married Elizabeth Douglas, daughter of Sir Robert Douglas of Glenbervie, New Zealand, who in 1911 published her two volume *The Family and Heirs of Sir Francis Drake*, the scholarly work on which all later accounts have been based. Her interest in her husband's family history extended to Buckland itself where she and Sir Francis returned to live in 1902 until his death in 1915. Here they maintained a lavishly appointed Edwardian house-hold. 'When the last Lady Drake drove from the Abbey to Yelverton, a pair of black horses drew her

carriage with two footmen on the box in dark-green uniforms turned out with white.'

Their only surviving child was a daughter, Elizabeth, who married in 1887 the Hon. John Colborne, later Lord Seaton, grandson of Field Marshal Lord Seaton, one of Wellington's generals and a Governor-General in Canada. They repaired the abbey once more, repointing the exterior, following removal of the rough cast applied in the eighteenth century, renewing the plumbing and above all creating the Chapel on the site of the old

(Opposite) Elizabeth, Lady Seaton in 1884, wearing the Drake pendant which also appears in Gheeraerts's portrait of her distant ancestor; painted by Edwin Long (Chapel Lobby; on loan from Plymouth Museums and Art Gallery). Lord and Lady Seaton inherited Buckland in 1915 and immediately carried out a major restoration programme. Her particular achievement was to create the Chapel on the site of the abbey high altar

In 1938 fire destroyed much of the upper floors of the abbey

high altar. A letter from Lady Seaton states, 'Mr. Snell, an architect did a good deal at Buckland Abbey' (H. J. Snell, a well-known Plymouth architect with a number of neo-Renaissance classical municipal buildings to his name).

The Seatons lived quietly. They had no children, and Buckland's valley site surrounded by trees and the old monastic walls helped ensure its isolation. On Lady Seaton's death in 1937 Captain Richard Owen Tapps-Gervis-Meyrick became the new owner. He was a descendant of the nineteenth-century Sir Thomas Fuller-Eliott-Drake's brother and the last member of the Drake family to live here, but only briefly. On 6 January 1938 a chimney flue caught fire which spread throughout the nave of the old church. The roof collapsed, causing terrible damage to the building, but the Drake treasures, including the drum, were saved. Repair work began immediately; but although structural restoration was completed within two years, the new fireproof floors, concrete beams and steel truss roof were more expedient than beautiful.

Two years later Captain Meyrick sold the west Devon part of the Buckland estate and in 1946 made plans to auction the abbey itself with its neighbouring land. Negotiations to preserve the abbey for the nation were intense, but shortly before the auction, Captain Arthur Rodd, a Yelverton landowner, bought the estate and presented the abbey, its garden, drive and lodge to the National Trust.

At that time the abbey enjoyed neither a collection nor an endowment, but mediation by the Trust with Plymouth City Council solved both problems. In 1951 the Council accepted a full repairing lease of the property from the National Trust (it was renewed in 1970) and converted the abbey into a branch of the City Museum and Art Gallery. The project was financed largely with grant aid from the Pilgrim Trust, supplemented by the fund-raising efforts of the Friends of Plymouth City Art Gallery and Buckland Abbey, a body which was founded for this specific purpose.

From 1951 to 1987 Buckland was administered by Plymouth as a Drake, Naval and West Country Folk Museum, stocked mainly with exhibits from the museum's collection. By the late 1970s however, it was realised that the displays needed rejuvenating, and the purchase by the National Trust in 1981 of the remainder of the Buckland estate from Captain Rodd's daughters provided the catalyst for reassessing both the presentation of Buckland Abbey and the relationship between the Trust and Plymouth. As a result, management of the abbey reverted to the National Trust, but with continued financial support from Plymouth, and two new exhibitions in the main galleries have been mounted by the museum.

In 1987 the property was closed to allow the abbey to be refurbished and the recently acquired Guesthouse to be converted into a centre for visitor facilities. It was reopened by the Countess Mountbatten on 19 July 1988, exactly 400 years after news that the Armada had been sighted off the Lizard had interrupted that legendary game of bowls on Plymouth Hoe.

This engraved-glass view of Buckland was commissioned from Simon Whistler in 1988 to celebrate the 400th anniversary of the defeat of the Spanish Armada

CHAPTER FOUR
THE ABBEY

THE APPROACH

In 1988 a new entrance was made for visitors to Buckland, but the original south-west Lodge and gate piers to the north east, built in 1804 by Lord Heathfield and enlarged in 1913, can still be seen. The car-park is linked to the property by a footpath created in 1988. During its construction an archaeological excavation was conducted in the field through which it passes. Slight traces of a building and medieval pottery were found, perhaps indicating the site of a monastic gatehouse, but overlaying the remains of an Iron Age circular-planned dwelling. To the right, but not open to the public, is the home farm.

At the end of the path a flight of steps leads into the first of several enclosures which were re-organised by William Marshall in the 1790s, and again in this century. This was probably a milking yard, as the early twentieth-century stone building ahead served as a cow shed until conversion into a schoolroom and lecture hall in 1989. Squeezed into the vestibule is a model of *The Golden Hind*, made for the 1953 Coronation procession in Birmingham. The lavatory block to the right was built as a stable that also dates from the early twentieth century.

THE GUESTHOUSE

Although this building is called the Monks' Guest-house, it seems likely that its original purpose was agricultural – designed with stabling below and a hayloft above at the east and west ends.

It was probably built in the early fourteenth century of local materials with a distinctive stone cornice and a series of granite buttresses intended to support the jointed cruck trusses of the roof. The windows were built as ventilation slits, but most have been enlarged since the fifteenth century, when conversion into living quarters for the monastery first occurred. It was certainly altered in the 1570s by Sir Richard Grenville, whose arms, with

The Guesthouse. Originally built as stabling, it was converted to domestic use and is now used as a shop and restaurant

those of his wife's family, St Leger, can be seen on the label stops above the south windows. The fireplace at the west end of what is now the restaurant also dates from this period. That to the east which uses cannibalised gate piers for jambs is probably later. Both fireplaces have the remains of ovens built into their sides.

By the end of the eighteenth century the Guest-house, described by William Marshall as a 'range of spacious office buildings', was beginning to lean towards the north and it required substantial extra internal buttressing and tying in with oak beams strapped with iron bars. Four of the oak ties remain visible in the west half of the building. Marshall also supervised the addition of a cottage on the west end and the outshot to the south. The smaller single-storey extension at the east end was built in the mid-nineteenth century and both extensions incorporate reused monastic material. In 1919 Lord Seaton is recorded as having turned the Guesthouse back into a cattle shed with tethering rings fixed to the south wall. Later a large grain silo filled the east end and a grain crusher and hopper were installed to the west.

The Guesthouse remained in agricultural use until 1988, when the National Trust restored the building to provide visitor facilities, a not unsuitable new use considering its history. Today the reception area with the kitchens below replace the silo, the restaurant has taken over the cattle shed and the shop the grain crusher. The west end cottage is once more an office.

THE OX SHEDS AND LINHAY

These are William Marshall's legacy, designed for the ox teams that worked at Buckland until 1881. 'Four aged oxen, or six growing steers, are the usual "plow" of the district', wrote Marshall, adding, they 'step out with a pace, which a Kentish clown would think a hardship to follow with his high-fed horse team'. In 1791 there were 22 oxen on the estate. In 1989 the sheds were restored for the use of craft workshops and a tea-room.

The sheds were built on a semi-octagonal plan enclosing a dung yard, through which an open rill passed, 'for the use of stock'. At the lower end of the yard there is an opening to another former straw yard, enclosed to one side by the east wall of the Great Barn. To the left is the nineteenth-century linhay, a traditional Devon building with an open-fronted cattle shed on the ground floor and a tallet (first floor) for fodder above. The fourth bay is wider than the others, possibly intended to house carts and agricultural machinery, which is its use today.

THE GREAT BARN

This is the finest and largest building at Buckland – a witness to the hugely successful farming enterprise pursued by the Cistercian monks. The buttressed walls are about 159 feet long, 32 feet wide, 40 feet high and 3 feet thick. They are punctuated by 23 broadly splayed ventilation openings and, high up around the interior, rows of putlog holes. Above these the oak roof is arch-braced and secured by curved collars, with mortice and tenoned joints united by wooden pegs. It may have been thatched originally.

Porches project on each side of the barn, both with an upper floor pigeon loft. When their doors were opened, the cross draught helped in winnowing the threshed corn which was 'thence flung, from hand to hand, to either end of the barn', being too narrow for wagons to turn inside. William Marshall

The Linhay

The Great Barn

(Opposite)
The eighteenth-century cider press in the Great Barn

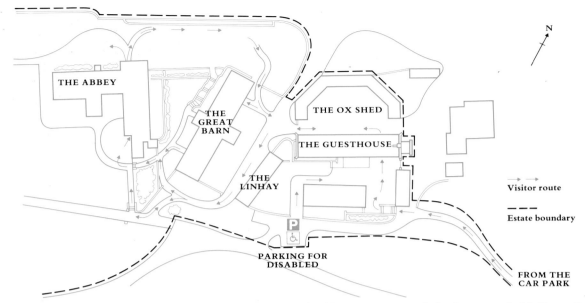

recognised the inconvenience of this method and in 1792 he was responsible for making three new doors, which allowed wagons to be driven the length of the building.

The barn floor was originally cobbled, but was concreted in the 1950s. Set into the concrete near the west porch are two millstones. Until about 1920 the abbey water-mill was here, powered by an underground stream which flowed between barn and abbey. A blocked door on the north side of the porch is all that now remains of the mill.

The cider press at the north end dates from the eighteenth century. By 1844 the estate included 27 acres of apple orchard and the gathered fruit, already pulped in a horse-operated crusher, was pressed beneath the top beam, originally wound down by a wooden screw and subsequently replaced by an iron screw dated 1815. The Buckland farm journals record the consumption in 1795 of 26 butts and one hogshead of cider (nearly 3,000 gallons).

In most Cistercian foundations, agricultural buildings were sited well away from the abbey church, but at Buckland the valley site may have dictated the barn's position nearby. This proved an advantage during the fourteenth century when French attacks threatened the outbreak of what became the Hundred Years War. The monks were granted a licence to crenellate and they built a fortified wall linking the barn to other monastic

buildings to create a defensive stronghold. Part of this wall remains at the south-east corner of the barn.

In 1941, during another war, the barn was requisitioned as a granary for the Admiralty. It was used for the last time in 1948, to store 1,000 tons of Manitoba wheat.

THE ABBEY

The Exterior

Compared to the great Cistercian abbeys of the twelfth century like Tintern, Fountains and Rievaulx, or the nave of Exeter Cathedral (an exact thirteenth-century contemporary), Buckland Abbey is of modest size – smaller in fact than the Great Barn. It is, nevertheless, a complex building to understand, particularly its original monastic function, which has been thoroughly disguised following conversion into a dwelling during the sixteenth century and subsequent alterations which have removed the other monastic buildings that once adjoined the church. Pictorial evidence prior to the eighteenth century is equally unhelpful, the only exception being a fifteenth-century drawing of the abbey in a map of Dartmoor depicting a

The south front of Buckland

church with a choir, nave and central tower, but no aisles and, apparently, no transepts (illustrated on page 9).

The first reliable reference appears in 1734, when Samuel and Nathaniel Buck engraved a view of the abbey from the north east. The print shows the north end of the Great Barn and, beyond it, formal walled gardens, the Tudor east wing, the crossing tower, a north transept and linking buildings to the turreted tower of the former abbot's lodgings. Since then the formal gardens have been simplified, the windows of the east wing gothicised and the north transept demolished. Also gone are the ancillary buildings, and all vestiges of the cloisters and chapter house which, on account of the lie of the land, were almost certainly to the north of the church. Demolition probably occurred in the 1800s, when S. P. Cockerell supervised major changes to the fabric, and indeed the external view of the abbey today, save for the renewed windows and the loss of the rough cast regularly applied in the eighteenth century to combat the weather, is virtually as Cockerell left it. Beyond the precinct wall, however, the turreted building shown in the engraving survives, now known as Tower Cottage (not open

to the public). This may have been the abbot's lodgings and became the abbey stable block, connected to the main building by a tunnel through which a bell system operated. Beyond it was the Cider House, now converted into a dwelling, and probably the several estate buildings listed in the 1834 inventory, such as the bakehouse, wash-house, brew-house and wood store.

THE KITCHEN WING

Visitors now approach the abbey from the south side. To the east is Grenville's kitchen wing, expanded in the eighteenth century to accommodate several comfortable panelled rooms on the second and third floors, now converted into flats. The wing still reveals the retaining arches of the chapels that once issued from the east wall of the south transept at ground-floor level. A door at the south end of the wing, currently the main entrance for visitors, is distinguished by the carved stone head of a crowned lady set into the tympanum. Judging by the four surrounding ribs, the head was the keystone in a vault; legend maintains the head forms the likeness of the abbey's founder, Amicia, Dowager Countess of Devon.

THE TOWER

Dominating the building is the crossing tower, unusually massive for a Cistercian abbey (their earliest churches had none), but the present undulating merlons, partially shown in the Buck engraving, are an eighteenth-century addition, which were followed by the curious brick flying buttress on the west flank that acts as a chimney flue. Clearly visible on the tower is the crease of the south transept roof above the crossing arch, filled in by Grenville when the transept was removed in order to light his new hall. The site of the transept is today a small yard, once known as the Bell Court, laid with river pebbles in about 1800.

THE PSEUDO-TRANSEPT

West of the tower is a short projecting wing, known as the pseudo-transept, built by Cockerell in the 1800s to provide a staircase and a new front door to the house, replacing an earlier version on the north side. At the Royal Academy in 1801 Cockerell exhibited an entrance for Buckland, 'designed as a seawalk and memorial' to Sir Francis Drake, which

The west front

may have been an earlier, and more extravagant front door than this sober gothick solution.

THE NAVE

This is now obscured by two mighty magnolia trees. The upper traceried windows, although fifteenth-century in style, are nineteenth-century replacements. Turn the corner and the nave's full height becomes apparent, still incorporating the voussoirs of earlier medieval openings and vestiges of its rough cast. Significantly, in that age of antiquarianism, Cockerell specified it should be tinted to resemble 'the Venerable Rust of an Abbey whose character and features denote the possession of many generations'.

THE NORTH FRONT

The north side of the abbey now reveals few traces of the transept, cloisters or their related buildings that dimly appear in the Buck engraving, and the wall beyond the yew trees opposite only discloses blocked openings of medieval origin. Instead there are two castelled porches. The smaller dates from the 1800s and has three carved insignia above the door fanlight: the open-hand badge of a baronetcy; the Drake shield bearing stars either side of a wavy line; and an esquire's helmet. The larger porch was previously a three-bay smoking room, the external door being a recent introduction.

THE EAST END

The east end of the abbey is a single wing built by Grenville to absorb the monastic chancel. The Buck engraving shows that this, like the north transept, had a castelled parapet above rectangular windows including two, each with three lights beneath drip-moulds, for the kitchen. These features were altered in the 1800s, when the parapet was removed, dormers added to light the servants' bedrooms, and several windows given gothick points and simple tracery. The wing is now virtually hidden by additional service rooms and tall yew hedges.

The Georgian Staircase

The Interior

THE ENTRANCE CORRIDOR

Entrance into the abbey is through the Amicia door, and immediately the transformation from a medieval monastic exterior to a Georgian domestic interior is apparent as the ecclesiastical scale of the former is reduced to a panelled corridor and balustered stairs.

On the right is a narrow curved passage (not open to visitors) that leads to a service staircase, and a small squint window with a view into the Tudor kitchen. Next, also on the right, is a granite corbel that supports an eighteenth-century fireplace in the room above, and a blocked door that once opened into the kitchen at gallery level. The corridor runs the length of the north–south wing which is clearly visible in the Buck engraving, but largely transformed during the 5th baronet's lifetime.

THE STAIRCASE

The 5th baronet was also responsible for the Staircase, which is one of the principal architectural features of the abbey. It rises through four floors with three turned balusters for each foliated scroll-ended tread. The gate at the half landing below was necessary to keep dogs from the upper floors.

On the second landing is a small medieval spiral staircase, now blocked after a few steps, but which originally led into the roof space of the church. Beyond it is a view of the thirteenth-century chancel arch. The stairs were oak grained in 1988.

The top landing led to the servants' quarters and a curious raised floor on the right. Traditionally, it is known as the tailor's bench, although whether or not it was used for this purpose is no longer certain. The staircase ahead (not open to visitors) leads to the tower room, which by 1832 had been converted into a pigeon house when the porthole windows of the belfry were reopened.

The door to the right may be that of the 'closet understair' mentioned in the 1834 inventory. Its contents shed some light on the unseen house-keeping labours in nineteenth-century Buckland. In addition to a brazure (sic), a perambulator and a bed warmer, there was a variety of specialised cleaning brushes for carpets, furniture, banisters, sweeping, scrubbing and black leading, besides a turk's head brush, two mops, a bucket and a dustpan.

The door to the left opens into the Four Lives Gallery. Above the door, in what was once the apex of the chancel crossing arch, is a trio of medieval foiled openings. There are signs that these were glazed and they would have therefore overlooked the chancel roof, when it was pitched lower than at present.

PICTURES

The Staircase is hung with prints showing views of the Plymouth area.

AT THE TOP OF THE STAIRS:

After JOHN ROBINSON (fl. 1715–45)
John Carteret, 2nd Earl Granville (1690–1763)
Dated 1744
Lord Granville is shown wearing his Garter robes. He held various offices of state including Secretary of State (1721–4 and 1742–6) and Lord President of the Council (from 1751 until his death). This is one of several portraits in the abbey on loan from Lord Clarendon and part of the large collection of portraits formed by the Clarendon family between the mid-seventeenth century and the early nineteenth century.

THE FOUR LIVES GALLERY

The Gallery extends the full length of the old abbey nave. By the nineteenth century the west end had been partitioned into bedrooms and the east end, under the tower, converted first into a laundry and later a chapel, but, according to Lady Drake, the Gallery was originally one room, no doubt used as a long gallery by the Tudor inhabitants and referred to as 'the great roof' by Cockerell. The 1938 fire seriously damaged the room and it was rebuilt using steel trusses that nevertheless convey an impression of medieval vaulting, of which only some springers survive.

DRAKE COATS OF ARMS

Apart from the bones of the vault, the only remaining architectural feature of importance is the granite fireplace within the north crossing arch, with its plaster overmantel bearing the Drake coat of arms. This depicts a ship, guided by the Divine Hand of Providence 'Auxilio Divino', above an open visor (indicating the family's rank as baronets),

The Drake coat of arms (Four Lives Gallery)

which rests on a shield symbolically bearing the two pole stars divided by the sea. The motto beneath, when translated, reads 'Great achievements from small beginnings'. The arms were inaccurately painted in the 1950s and will be cleaned when resources permit.

On the left side of the overmantel is a second coat of arms and the date 1655 above the initials R.N. The arms belong to the Drakes, but the owner of the initials remains a mystery. On the opposite side are two more shields, one apparently depicting a drake, swimming, and the other the arms of Gregory, a reference to Elizabeth Gregory, wife of Sir Francis's brother Thomas.

EXHIBITION

In 1951 the Gallery was set up as a naval museum, but with the reorganisation of Buckland in 1988 the history of the entire property has been displayed here, divided into four periods: Medieval Monastery, Tudor Mansion, Georgian Home and The National Trust; hence 'The Four Lives' title to the exhibition.

Everything on show is described and the abbey's history traced from its foundations in 1278 until 1988. Among the exhibits are fragments of the monastic era, including stone tracery, capitals and floor tiles; the documents by which John Hele and Christopher Harris conveyed the abbey to Sir Francis Drake; the first edition of William Mar-

shall's *The Rural Economy of the West of England* (1796); and photographs of the 1938 fire. Artistic impressions of the pre-Dissolution buildings and a model to illustrate Grenville's conversion of the abbey into a house, help explain the development of Buckland.

THE STAIRS

These occupy the short south wing known as the Pseudo-Transept. The wing was built by Cockerell in the 1790s to create a suitably imposing framework for a new front door. Its predecessor on the north front had proved inconvenient, since 'one goes down [the] hill merely to enter [the] hall to go up a staircase of 32 steps to the Habitable Rooms'. Cockerell's stairs were partly destroyed in 1938 and replaced by the present fireproof concrete version, when the plaster on the walls was also removed.

ENGRAVED GLASS

The three-light window on the half-landing contains four engraved glass panels to commemorate the 400th anniversary of the Armada's defeat. The panels were commissioned by the National Trust from the artist Simon Whistler.

PICTURES

After JOHN SEYMOUR LUCAS (1849–1923)
'The Armada is in Sight'
Dated 1880
Engraving
Possibly the most famous story of the Drake legend concerns the game of bowls played on Plymouth Hoe on the afternoon of 19 July 1588. When Drake was warned of the Armada's approach, he allegedly remarked, 'We have time to finish the game and beat the Spaniards too'. Seymour Lucas was a leading history painter of the 1870s and '80s, whose work was appreciated by chauvinistic Victorians, busily engaged on building the British Empire.

ENGLISH SCHOOL, 17TH CENTURY
Sir Nicholas Bacon (1509–79)
Bacon was appointed Lord Keeper of the Great Seal in 1558 by Elizabeth I. This is a copy probably commissioned by the 1st Earl of Clarendon of the anonymous 1579 portrait of Bacon, one version of which is in the National Portrait Gallery.

'The burial of Admiral Drake', by Thomas Davidson (on loan from Plymouth Museums and Art Gallery)

THOMAS DAVIDSON (fl. 1863–1903)
The Burial of Admiral Drake
Drake was aged about 50 when he died during the raid on Spanish territories in the Caribbean. He was buried at sea off Nombre de Dios on 28 January 1596.

THE DRAKE GALLERY

The Gallery is the principal room on the first floor, introduced by Grenville in the 1570s as part of the horizontal division of the nave. In the nineteenth century it was further divided into a bedroom and two dressing-rooms, but the room divisions were destroyed by the 1938 fire and never replaced. It is now devoted to an exhibition on the life of Sir Francis Drake, which includes some of the most precious of the Drake relics (described clockwise round the room).

PICTURES

Attributed to FEDERIGO ZUCCARO (1543–1609)
Elizabeth I (1533–1603)
Elizabeth is shown standing in front of a throne, her right hand resting on the Royal Orb. Behind the throne is a tapestry bearing the Royal Arms and the partly visible motto of the Order of the Garter, 'On y [honi] soit qui mal y pense'. Zuccaro came to

England from Rome in 1575. He made two drawings of Queen Elizabeth (both in the British Museum), but returned to Italy the same year and it remains uncertain if he painted any of the portraits of Elizabeth now attributed to him.

ENGLISH SCHOOL, 16TH CENTURY
Francis Drake as a young man

MARCUS GHEERAERTS THE YOUNGER (1561–1636)
Sir Francis Drake (c.1545–96)
Painted after 1590
Gheeraerts was a Huguenot refugee and portrait specialist.

Attributed to GEORGE GOWER (1540–96)
Elizabeth Sydenham, Lady Drake (d.1598)
Painted in 1585
The second Lady Drake was the daughter of Sir George Sydenham of Coombe Sydenham, Somerset. She married Sir Francis in 1584/5 and after his death Sir William Courtenay of Powderham Castle, Devon. She died childless. The portrait shows her wearing the jewelled locket containing Queen Elizabeth's portrait miniature by Nicholas Hilliard, presented by the Queen to Drake in 1581. Gower was Serjeant Painter to Elizabeth I from 1581. He worked largely on decorative painting in the royal palaces.

John Seymour Lucas (1849–1923)
The Surrender of Don Pedro de Valdés to Sir Francis Drake

On 21 July 1588 Francis Drake seized the crippled Spanish ship *Nuestra Señora del Rosario* off Start Point, Devon. Aboard was the commander Don Pedro, who was entertained by Drake on his own ship, the *Revenge*, before being interrogated and sent to London as a prisoner. Three years later Drake received some £3,000 ransom money for the Spanish commander.

DRAKE EXHIBITS

The Royal Standards

Two sixteenth-century flags bearing the Royal Arms, perhaps flown on board *The Golden Hind* at Deptford when Drake was knighted in April 1581. The smaller flag is made of plain silk, the larger of Spanish brocade, and both are emblazoned in gold. The green and white fringe represents the Queen's personal colours.

'Sir Francis Drake Revived'

This account of Drake's adventures in the West Indies was edited and published by his nephew in 1626.

The Drake 'Lodestone'

A sixteenth-century lodestone set in a silver mount of *c*.1700. It was reputedly given by Drake to Laurence Kemeys, an associate of Sir Walter Ralegh.

The Drake Cup

A silver gilt cup engraved with a version of Mercator's world map of 1587. It was made by Abraham Gessner of Zurich and may have been given by Drake to his friend, Sir Anthony Rous of Halton, Cornwall.

Drake's Drum

A late sixteenth-century side drum painted with Drake's coat of arms. It is one of the oldest surviving in Europe, and may be one of thirteen bought for £17 in 1595 for use on Drake's last voyage. The drum was seen at Buckland by the traveller George Lipscombe in 1799 and may well have been kept here throughout the last 400 years. According to legend, the drum will beat of its own accord to summon Drake back from the dead, if ever England is in danger. But the legend dates mainly from the publication in 1896 of Sir Henry Newbolt's ballad 'Drake's Drum'.

Letters patent of Queen Elizabeth I to Sir Francis Drake

The document, dated 15 March 1587, commis-

One of the sixteenth-century colours used by Drake's regiment of soldiers

sioned Drake to command a fleet which successfully attacked Spanish shipping in Cadiz harbour on 19 April 1587 – the famous episode when he 'singed the King of Spain's beard'.

The Drake Colours

Two from a set of six regimental colours used in the sixteenth century by Drake's own trained band of soldiers. They are the oldest and only complete set of their kind. The colours are made of silk taffeta painted in gold.

Drake's Munitions 1587–8

The list of ammunition and hand weapons supplied to Sir Francis Drake and his ships from 'Her Majesty's store' prior to the Armada.

Sir Francis Drake's expenses in 1588

This document, written by Drake's secretary James Bodenham, is annotated by Lord Burghley, the Lord Chancellor of England.

The Armada Medals

Five English and Dutch medals commemorating the defeat of the Armada, the first historical event for which medals were struck in England.

Finds from Spanish Shipwrecks

28 ships from the Spanish Armada were wrecked off the Irish coast. Underwater excavations have produced many finds including the relics shown here.

THE DRAKE CHAMBER

Despite its association with Drake, the presence of the Grenville arms in the fireplace spandrels indicates this room predates Sir Francis. Less secure, however, is the date of the panelling which fits uneasily, particularly around the windows, and the frieze which seems too precisely carved for sixteenth-century work. Panelling certainly existed in the house in the eighteenth century, since Cockerell recommended, 'the oak wainscoting of the West Room be Rubbed or brushed over with oil varnish', and it can be dimly seen in the early nineteenth-century watercolour now hanging in the room. One tradition suggests the panelling was brought here by Lord Heathfield in the 1790s, another that Grenville imported it from Stowe, his house in Cornwall. Whatever its origin, it was removed after the 1938 fire, repaired and refitted, which may account for its present trimmed appearance. The ceiling was also repaired in the 1950s, but with no pretence at restoration.

A compelling attraction of the room is the view from the west window overlooking the Tavy valley. During the eighteenth century it was used as a drawing-room, particularly by the ladies of the house. The watercolour shows two of them seated near the south window, although this too is a replacement following the destruction of its predecessor during the Civil War. This may also be the drawing-room described in the 1834 inventory containing, 'ten Vols of Marshall's Agriculture bound in Russia' (a type of leather) and a portrait of Sir Francis Drake. Since 1951 the room has been presented as a dining-room, using oak furniture brought in from elsewhere, but matching a description in 1846 by the visitor Rachel Evans who wrote, 'the furniture in general was ancient and time worn'.

PICTURES

ENGLISH, 19TH CENTURY
Buckland Abbey c.1830
Watercolour
A sketch of the drawing-room.

ENGLISH, 16TH CENTURY
An unknown Tudor gentleman
The portrait bears a likeness to the young Edward VI.

ENGLISH, 16TH CENTURY
Portrait of an unidentified Elizabethan lady

ENGLISH, 16TH CENTURY
Portrait of a Tudor gentleman
Said to be Charles Brandon, Duke of Suffolk, who died in 1545. He was a favourite of Henry VIII and combined a successful military career with the office of Marshal of the Royal Household. Like the Grenvilles, he was a considerable beneficiary of land distributed after the Dissolution of the Monasteries.

Circle of MARCUS GHEERAERTS THE YOUNGER (1561–1636)
An unknown Elizabethan lady, said to be Queen Elizabeth I
*c.*1610
The only clue to the identity of the sitter is the curious symbolic globe in the bottom left-hand corner.

ENGLISH SCHOOL, 17TH CENTURY
Anne Carew
Dated 1606
Anne, daughter of Sir Peter and Lady Carew, was wife of Sir Allen Apsley, Lieutenant of the Tower of London.

MARCUS GHEERAERTS THE YOUNGER (1561–1636)
Sir Henry Palmer (d.1611)
Dated 1586
Palmer was the distinguished commander of the *Antelope* during the Armada campaign and took part in the Battle of Gravelines; he was subsequently Controller of the Navy (1598–1611).

The Drake Chamber

FURNITURE

A sixteenth-century Italian oak cassone or chest, carved on the front with a central panel depicting Venus and a satyr with Cupid, flanked by two figures on each side, possibly representing the Four Seasons.

A sixteenth-century French oak clothes press, the two doors panelled and carved with grotesque heads.

A sixteenth-century oak chest, the front carved with the figures of saints carrying their attributes.

A nineteenth-century oak settle in gothic style, possibly made up from sixteenth-century pieces.

Five late seventeenth-century walnut high-backed chairs.

A late sixteenth-century oak court cupboard.

A late sixteenth-century oak sideboard.

An early seventeenth-century oak refectory table.

THE GEORGIAN DINING ROOM

At the opposite end of the Drake Gallery is this chaste eighteenth-century room, very different from the dark panelled rooms of its Tudor predecessors. It was fitted out by Sir Francis Henry, 5th Baronet, after the death of his mother, a life tenant, in 1768. Panelling was reduced to a simple dado and doors surmounted by a bolection moulding. (The dado to south and west is a twentieth-century replacement of the original destroyed by dry rot.)

The Georgian Dining Room

On the reverse of a board to the left of the fireplace, the only Tudor feature left, is a red pencilled inscription, 'Mr Thomas Rowe 19th April, 1772, Master of this Job and Foreman of the Sawyers', thereby precisely dating the refit. Surprisingly, Mr Rowe also tactfully managed to incorporate a reminder of the monastic church: a carved corbel figure of the ox of St Luke in the north-east corner. By 1800, when Cockerell was employed to modernise the house, this room was known as the new eating room. He recorded how it was hung with a green flock wallpaper, by then beginning to age, and he recommended 'a general new paper with a plainness of character . . . rather a light colour, but of a clothy warm appearance and the dadoes to be painted somewhat in tone with the paper to be given an appearance of heighth'. In 1988 the room was repainted to achieve a similar effect.

In 1834 the room was equipped with twelve mahogany chairs with leather seats, six elbow chairs and, as was often then the practice, four wainscot dining-tables that could be moved into the centre of the room as required. It is now furnished with a single dining-table with chairs drawn up to it rather than placed against the dado rail.

PICTURES

JOHN OPIE RA (1761–1807)
Anne Bellett
Known as 'the Cornish wonder', Opie was a child prodigy who made his fortune in London painting Rembrandtesque portraits and historical subjects.

JOHN OPIE RA (1761–1807)
John Bellett junior

SIR EDWARD HAMILTON
John Bellett

JAMES NORTHCOTE RA (1746–1831)
Captain G. Rous
The Rous family came from St Dominick in Cornwall. In the sixteenth century Sir Anthony Rous had been a friend and executor to Sir Francis Drake. Northcote was a Devon-born painter who had trained under Sir Joshua Reynolds.

JAMES NORTHCOTE RA (1746–1831)
Leonard Troughear Holmes

THOMAS BUTTERWORTH (1768–1842)
Loss of the West Indiaman 'Bellim'
The *Bellim* was wrecked in a gale on the Goodwin Sands on 4 November 1804, when homeward bound from the West Indies.

NICHOLAS POCOCK (1740–1821)
The East Indiaman 'Dutton' wrecked in Plymouth Sound
The *Dutton* was lost in a storm on rocks beneath the Citadel in 1796.

S. BAKER
A Naval Engagement
The painting dates from before 1790 and shows an English 36-gun frigate in action against its French counterpart.

FURNITURE

An early nineteenth-century mahogany six-leaf concertina dining-table on eight gadrooned legs, sometimes known as a naval table.

A set of nine mid-eighteenth-century mahogany dining-chairs by Thomas Chippendale (on loan from Mr Thomas Whipham) and a further three in the style of Chippendale.

A mid-eighteenth-century mahogany semi-circular card-table with a folding top.

An early nineteenth-century mahogany bow-front sideboard in the Sheraton style.

A late eighteenth-century mahogany bow-front sideboard cross-banded in kingwood.

A late eighteenth-century mahogany tilt-top wine-table with scalloped edge.

A late eighteenth-century mahogany and brass-bound wine cooler.

An early nineteenth-century mahogany and brass-bound cellaret.

Two silver tea urns hallmarked London 1778/9.

A cream ware punchbowl transfer-printed with masonic emblems.

A cream ware jug transfer-printed with masonic emblems.

THE GEORGIAN CORRIDOR

The corridor is lit by a large south-facing fifteenth-century-style window. In the south-east corner is a sculpted corbel representing the eagle of the evangelist St John, a companion to the ox of St Luke in the Dining Room. Together with the now lost corbel figures of a man (St Matthew) and a lion (St Mark), the four would have supported the crossing vault beneath the tower.

The contents of the corridor relate mainly to eighteenth- and nineteenth-century members of the family, in particular the display case which contains an assortment of personal things, including Lady Fuller-Eliott-Drake's travelling case.

PICTURES

REV. JOHN SWETE (1752–1821)
The Great Barn

JOHN WHITE ABBOTT (1763–1851)
The Great Barn
Watercolour *c*.1800

SCULPTURE

General George Augustus Eliott, Lord Heathfield of Gibraltar (1717–90)
Bronzed plaster, 1801
Lord Heathfield was a distinguished soldier, who made his name by successfully defending Gibraltar against siege by the Spanish between 1779 and 1783. To the right hangs an engraving of Lord Heathfield's portrait by Sir Joshua Reynolds, which is in the National Gallery. Reynolds imagined him at the height of the Gibraltar siege, with the key to the Rock in his hand.

FURNITURE

An early nineteenth-century mahogany snap-top breakfast table.

An eight-day longcase clock by Thomas Hunter of London in a walnut case.

THE PYM GALLERY

MURALS

The gallery is named after the series of four mural paintings specially commissioned for Buckland Abbey by Lord and Lady Astor as part of the Festival of Britain celebrations in 1951. The artist was Roland Pym, a mural specialist who, in 1953, painted the Queen's Room at Westminster Abbey for the coronation. Two of the murals represent the battle against the Armada in July 1588; a third shows Sir Francis Drake in the course of his voyage around the world between 1577 and 1580; and the last, originally intended as an overdoor, portrays Drake's ship, *The Golden Hind*.

'A Royal Game', by Sir William Reynolds-Stephens, depicts a symbolic game of chess between Elizabeth I and Philip II of Spain. (Tate Gallery bronze, which is based on the plaster at Buckland)

SCULPTURE

Sir William Reynolds-Stephens PRSBS (1862–1943)
A Royal Game
Bronzed plaster
It depicts an imaginary game of chess in which Queen Elizabeth I pits her wits, and ships, against a devious Philip II of Spain. Elizabeth has won the game, just as the English repelled the Armada, leaving Philip holding one of his bishops. Reynolds-Stephens explained, 'I tried to give Elizabeth's character of self assurance ... on the other hand I have shown Philip II in an attitude of grab ...' The sculpture was the model for a bronze edition, exhibited first at the Royal Academy in 1911 and now in the Tate Gallery, London.

EXHIBITION

The room also contains an exhibition devoted to four principal topics illustrating the legends that have enhanced Sir Francis Drake's reputation in the last four hundred years. These are: the creation of the leat that brought water to the City of Plymouth; the Drum and its ghostly percussions; the pioneering voyage around the world; and the many anniversaries commemorating Drake's

achievements, especially the Armada Quatercentenary of 1988.

THE LANDING

Four more portraits from the Clarendon Collection hang here.

English School
William Camden (1551–1623)
Camden, the antiquary and historian, published his *Britannia* (a survey of the British Isles) in 1586 and the first part of *Annals of the Reign of Elizabeth I* in 1615. This portrait is a copy of the anonymous original dated 1622, which is in Worcester College, Oxford.

After John de Critz the Elder (c.1554–1642)
Thomas Sackville, 1st Earl of Dorset (1536–1608)
Sackville was both poet and statesman, assuming the position of Lord Treasurer in 1599. In 1586 he announced the death sentence to Mary Queen of Scots. One example of the prototype portrait of Sackville, on which this copy is based, is at Knole in Kent.

English School
Lancelot Andrews (1555–1626)
Andrews was Chaplain in Ordinary to Elizabeth I and successively Bishop of Chichester, Ely and Winchester. He assisted in drafting the new authorised version of the Bible in 1611.

English School
Thomas Egerton, Viscount Brackley (1540–1617)
Egerton was a lawyer and statesman who carried out many diplomatic missions for Queen Elizabeth I. He was made Lord Chancellor in 1603.

THE GREAT HALL

The Great Hall is positioned within the original crossing area of the church, directly beneath the tower and adjacent to the south transept that was demolished by Grenville to bring light to this, the most lavishly remodelled room in his conversion. Its chief glory is the decorative plasterwork of the ceiling and frieze, and an overmantel incorporating the Roman numerals MCCCCLXXVI (1576), an early date for plasterwork of this quality in Devon.

In the mid-nineteenth century the hall was equipped with a billiard table, but later photographs show it hung with family portraits, furnished with a

The Great Hall

grand piano and the most precious heirlooms from the estate of the great Sir Francis, including his sword and shield above the screen and his drum and banners against the window wall. Today the room is furnished in a style contemporary with the sixteenth century.

PLASTERWORK

The ceiling, with its interlocking ribs, angle fleurons and two pendants, was restored after the fire, but the rest survived as Grenville's legacy. At the west end an allegorical scene symbolises his retirement from a military career to the cloistered surroundings of Buckland. In the pastoral scene a knight rests under a vine, weapons piled and his horse tethered. His shield and a skull hang from the tree of life. This, like the vast majority of early Devon plasterwork, was never coloured, relying on the play of light on limewash to throw up the relief. Exceptionally, traces of colour have been found on the overmantel shields and the four figures representing the four cardinal virtues. They are: *Justice holding the scales, Temperance diluting wine with water, Fortitude entwined by a snake* and *Prudence holding a book* [the

Scriptures]. Above them, three shield-bearing satyrs disguise the ceiling trusses.

The frieze on the east wall includes an elaborate strapwork cartouche supporting three hanging shields. Beneath it, and running around the room, a plaster leaf scroll completes the ensemble.

PANELLING AND SCREEN

Three walls of the room are oak panelled between fluted pilasters. The panels are unusually large and may have been brought from another Drake house on the Meavy estate. All around the room an inlaid frieze of holly and boxwood is divided up by carved animal masks and figures in various attitudes, including a musician and sheila-na-gigs (fertility figures).

Behind the panelling are traces of stone columns from the old church, and it is possible that the solid west wall was once the medieval pulpitum. Sadly, the original timber screen at the east end was rebuilt in brick during the nineteenth century.

FIREPLACE

The broad granite fireplace with upturned centre and a herringbone pattern of slate at the back is typical of the sixteenth century.

FLOOR

This was laid with pink and white triangular patterned tiles, perhaps imported from Holland. Their level is some 18 inches above the floor of the Cistercian abbey, beneath which remain the graves of monks who were buried in the nave.

PICTURES

After MARCUS GHEERAERTS THE YOUNGER (1561–1636)
William Cecil, 1st Baron Burghley (1520–98)
Burghley rose to become Queen Elizabeth's chief minister in the latter years of her reign. He is shown wearing the garter robes with the great collar and badge pendant of St George and carrying the white rod that denotes the office of Lord High Treasurer. He was Secretary of State (1550–3 and 1558–72) and Lord High Treasurer (1572–98). The portrait may be a seventeenth-century copy of a version at Hatfield House, Hertfordshire, which bears the same inscription. From the Clarendon Collection.

After JOHN DE CRITZ THE ELDER (*c*.1554–1642)
Robert Cecil, 1st Earl of Salisbury (1563–1612)
Cecil succeeded his father, Lord Burghley, as Elizabeth's chief minister. He is shown wearing the garter robes and carries the white rod of the Lord High Treasurer. He was Secretary of State (1596–1608) and Lord High Treasurer in 1606. A Clarendon copy of the portrait at Hatfield, the house he built in 1607–11.

FURNITURE

A pair of late seventeenth-century walnut and cane-back chairs.

A sixteenth-century oak chest in the gothic style.

A nineteenth-century oak armchair with an arcaded back, copied from an older version in the Bodleian Library, Oxford, said to be made from timbers of *The Golden Hind.*

A seventeenth-century-style oak chest with a carved front and grotesque masks on either corner.

A late seventeenth-century Portuguese chestnut frame chair upholstered in tooled leather.

Two sixteenth-century Venetian sweet chestnut chairs with painted and gilded decoration.

A nineteenth-century copy of a chair said to have been made from the timbers of Drake's 'The Golden Hind'

A sixteenth-century-style oak altar table with a carved frieze and cup and cover legs.

An early seventeenth-century oak armchair with carved panelling and inset marquetry.

A late sixteenth-century Chatham chest bound with iron strapwork.

A late sixteenth-century oak refectory table with gadrooned frieze and cup and cover legs.

An oak refectory table with drawleaf top, inlaid frieze and cup and cover legs.

A pair of iron chandeliers commissioned by the National Trust in 1988.

THE CHAPEL

The restoration of this chapel in 1917 on the site of the abbey's high altar is recorded by a brass plaque on the west wall. Previously the room had been used as the servants' hall, but when a painted medieval column was accidentally discovered behind the room's eighteenth-century panelling, Lady Seaton organised a full-scale investigation. A Tudor stone doorway was uncovered and the floor excavated to a depth of 2 feet, revealing fragments of fourteenth-century glazed tiles portraying, amongst other patterns, a fish and 'a rather nice little dragon'.

The recessed splays of the great east window and windows each side of the altar were revealed, and within the north wall the original aumbry was found still in position. Buried in the former fireplace in the south wall were the remains of the piscina, now restored, and enough pieces of a three-bay sedilia to enable two miniature lierne vaults beneath traceried arches to be rebuilt. Other carved stones, probably from the reredos, were reassembled beneath the altar table. Most tantalising of all were the empty graves at the foot of the altar, including perhaps Amicia's own.

The Chapel was rededicated to St Benedict and the Blessed Virgin Mary, and Lady Seaton's efforts were rewarded when she obtained a licence to celebrate mass (now hanging left of the altar), issued by Pope Pius XV on 15 November 1917. From 1951 to 1987 the Chapel housed a collection of West Country ecclesiastical silver, but it has once more been furnished as a chapel.

The Chapel

FURNISHINGS

Four early twentieth-century electroliers. Purchased in 1987 by the National Trust from the parish church at Uffculme, east Devon.

A granite holy water stoup. Originally a household mortar, the stoup was set on a reclaimed medieval shaft by Lady Seaton.

A nineteenth-century oak pew.

Two early seventeenth-century oak highback chairs.

Stained glass. Said to be from Rheims Cathedral, rescued by Lord and Lady Seaton after the First World War.

A silver thirteenth-century altar cross. Originally studded with precious stones, but desecrated, probably at the time of the Dissolution. It was presented to Buckland by Lord Mount Edgcumbe.

The Holy Bible. These two volumes, dated 1717, belonged to the Hole family of Parke, Bovey Tracey, Devon.

An oak armchair. In gothic style, probably made up from fifteenth-century pieces.

A font. Presented by the Rector of Holy Trinity, Exeter, to his church in 1855. The church was deconsecrated in 1968 and the font acquired by the National Trust in 1989.

Two carved oak beams. Hung high on the walls, they were brought here from elsewhere in the abbey after the fire.

THE KITCHEN

The monastic kitchen would have been sited an inconvenient distance from Grenville's newly converted Great Hall and so a new kitchen was built within the angle of the south transept and chancel, allowing easy access to the screens passage.

In 1846 Rachel Evans, an early Buckland tourist, wrote about the kitchen, 'an epicure might have been charmed by the numerous stores arranged around to prepare the costly viandes for his table'. By then the dining-room had moved upstairs and Cockerell had converted a series of smaller rooms near the Kitchen for the housekeeper and butler, and provided others each with a special purpose: china and glass rooms, boot room, butler's pantry, scullery, dairy and store room, besides burrowing into the ground to the east to create cellars. A small

The two little vaults beneath traceried arches were reconstructed from fragments found by Lady Seaton during her recreation of the Chapel earlier in this century

room behind the settle is still used for storing wood and faggots necessary for keeping all the fires alight.

In 1950 the Kitchen was furnished as a tea-room for visitors, but in 1989 it was restored to its original purpose and the walls repainted in the traditional pink limewash.

HEARTHS

The room is dominated by two open hearths. That to the south is earlier, with a massive granite lintel constructed beneath a relieving arch. Above it are eight pairs of brackets for spit rods and a hoisting wheel, possibly used for turning the spit, but more likely for lifting sides of bacon and ham on to hooks ranged along the ceiling brackets.

The later west hearth has two built-in bread ovens, but during the eighteenth century it became outmoded and was blocked up, to be replaced by a row of brick charcoal ovens, a French invention known as stewing stoves. These comprised six recessed iron plates that were heated with charcoal. The ashes fell through to the iron shelf below, and fresh charcoal was kept on the lower level. In 1950 the old hearth was revealed during investigations into a damp patch that had appeared on this inside wall. According to tradition the antlers above the hearth came from a stag that once chased Sir Francis Drake up a tree. He had his revenge by shooting the stag and mounting the antlers here.

CONTENTS

The Kitchen is provided with utensils of various dates, many of them of traditional design which changed little over the years. They have all been brought to Buckland from elsewhere, but the 1834 inventory mentions many similar items, notably the spits and large centre table. Roasting meats on the spits was supplemented by stewing or boiling food in cauldrons and kettles suspended from hooks above the fire. One kettle is hung on a tilting device known as a 'lazy maid'. It enabled the kitchen staff to pour hot water without burning their hands. Food was stored in pottery jars like those against the east wall, ranging in size from small stoneware pots for preserves, to large earthenware or cloam crocks for bread. Some of the equipment for preparing food is on the tables – a wooden potato masher, hinged lemon squeezers, scissor-like nippers for cutting sugar from sugar loaves, and pestles and mortars for pounding ingredients together. China is stacked up on the dresser and more crockery, pewter tankards, brass and copper cooking vessels are shelved on the west wall.

THE CHAPEL LOBBY

Originally part of the abbey choir and later the screens passage linking the Tudor kitchen to the Great Hall, the lobby is now the exit corridor for visitors. In the eighteenth century an oak dog gate was added at the stairs' end. At the opposite end the lobby opens into a small room, once a chapel off the north transept which retains the only medieval vault remaining in the abbey. It was used as a smoking room at the beginning of this century and now contains information on the Buckland Abbey Appeal.

PICTURE

EDWIN LONG RA (1829–91)
Elizabeth Beatrice Drake, later Lady Seaton (d.1937)
Dated 1884
Lady Seaton was the only child of Sir Francis George Augustus Fuller-Eliott-Drake. She married the Hon. John Reginald Upton Colborne, later the 2nd Lord Seaton, in 1887. They succeeded to the abbey in 1915 and immediately began restoring it,

suffering in the process from the familiar inconveniences of building work. On 2 October 1917, Lady Seaton wrote, 'Buckland is uninhabitable without its hot water frequently, if not every day'. Her more enduring achievement is the restoration of the Chapel.

EXIT

From the abbey a right turn takes visitors back towards the reception area. The route follows an avenue of ancient yews, some badly damaged in the great storms of January 1990. The wall to the north probably formed part of the monastic buildings, shown in the Buck engraving extending towards the abbot's lodgings. Evidence of blocked openings and reused granite quoins extends along its length. To the right, another low wall hides a shady lawn, reputedly the site of the monks' graveyard; but, like much else at Buckland, it has never been excavated, so its true purpose remains a secret.

The herb garden

CHAPTER FIVE
THE GARDEN

This is largely a twentieth-century creation, which effectively disguises any medieval foundations, and bears no resemblance to the walled enclosures and circular pond illustrated in the Buck engraving of 1734. Such formality may have had Tudor origins, but an intriguing reference in a household account book for 1709 refers to a payment to 'ye French Gardener', which equally may explain such an ordered plan. Unfortunately, the fate of that garden is unknown, and there was no apparent trace of it by the time William Marshall visited in 1791, when he commented only on the encircling gloom of the overgrown land. Doubtless the yew avenue north of the abbey was part of that bosky landscape described in the 1946 sale catalogue as 'the second oldest in England'. Sadly it was badly damaged in the January gale of 1990 and subsequently has had to be quite drastically reduced.

Engravings of nineteenth-century Buckland invariably show the abbey's south-west elevation romantically wreathed in climbers and surrounded by trees, perhaps planted by the 5th Baronet who was known to be interested in forestry. The effect was judged 'most picturesque' by Rachel Evans in her guidebook to Tavistock (first published in 1846). She was also amazed at the vast size of the trees in the garden. She may have been referring to cedars now gone, or to the large Pine and *Picea smithiana*, which had to be felled in 1989. Today the south elevation is dominated by two vast magnolias, *M. delavayi* to the west, a species introduced to this country from China in 1899 and probably planted here by Lady Seaton, and *M. grandiflora* from the south-east United States, planted since 1951.

The level lawn north west of the abbey also probably dates from the Seatons' time; it was originally used for croquet and now for the occasional game of bowls.

In 1916 Lady Seaton employed a Mr Thessiger to carry out some landscaping, the extent of which is unknown. The existing shrubs date only from the 1950s, when a formidable team of advisers to the National Trust made their mark. They included Sir Henry Studholme of Wembury, the Viscountess Astor, Lord Mount Edgcumbe and Vita Sackville-West. Their recommendations included the removal of several trees and large numbers of ponticum rhododendrons, bamboos and laurels, then regarded as 'far too Victorian for Buckland'. To replace them, 'choice shrubs' including Eucryphias, Camellias, Hydrangeas, evergreen Azaleas and Japanese Acers were planted. The prominent climber *Aristolochia macrophylla* (Dutchman's Pipe) was almost certainly planted at the same date to grow over a large Box specimen in the north-west corner.

It is probable that the Herb Garden west of the medieval Great Barn was established after a visit by Vita Sackville-West. The irregular-shaped dwarf Box-edged beds contain over 40 different herbs, including Feverfew, Comfrey, Rosemary, Thyme, Fennel and Lad's Love, which have been grown for centuries for their medicinal properties.

A view of the house from the Great Barn

BIBLIOGRAPHY

PRIMARY SOURCES

The bulk of the surviving Drake family papers are in the Devon Record Office in Exeter, augmented by others in the West Devon Record Office in Plymouth and the Meyrick archive which is held mainly by the family agents in Exeter. Recent history and copies of the Devon Record Office material, with some analysis of its contents, are held by Plymouth Museum.

SECONDARY SOUCES

ARBER, Edward (Ed.), *The Last Fight of The Revenge at Sea*, London, 1901.

BARBER, B.J., *Buckland Abbey*, York University undergraduate study, 1984.

BARBER, James, 'Sir Francis Drake's Investment in Plymouth Property', *Transactions of the Devonshire Association*, cxiii, 1981.

BETTLEY, Tom, *Report on the archaeological and architectural investigation of the Guesthouse*, 1988.

BRITTON, John, *Devonshire Illustrated*, 1832.

BUCK, Samuel and Nathaniel, *Antiquities*, i, 1734.

COPELAND, G.W., 'Some problems of Buckland Abbey', *Transactions of the Devon Association*, lxxxv, 1953.

CORBETT, Julian, *Sir Francis Drake*, London, 1890.

Country Life, xxix, 1916.

CUMMING, Alex, *Buckland Abbey*, 1981.

ELIOTT-DRAKE, Lady, *The Family and Heirs of Sir Francis Drake*, 2 Vols, 1911.

EVANS, Rachel, *Tavistock and its Vicinity*, 1846.

GILL, Crispin, *Buckland Abbey*, 1968.

HORN, Pamela, *William Marshall*, 1982.

MARSHALL, William, *The Rural Economy of the West of England*, 2 vols, 1796.

PYE, Andrew, *Report on excavation of the Cider House garden*, 1984.

ROWSE, A.L., *Sir Richard Grenville of the Revenge*, London, 1937.

ROWE, J. Brooking, 'The Cistercian Houses of Devon', *Transactions of the Devonshire Association*, vii, 1875–6.

SUGDEN, John, *Sir Francis Drake*, 1990.

TIPPING, Henry A., *English Homes*, Period 3, ii, 1927.

WORTH, R.N., *Calendar of the Plymouth Municipal Records*, Plymouth, 1893.

YOUINGS, Joyce, 'Drake, Grenville and Buckland Abbey', *Transactions of the Devon Association*, cxii, 1980.

INDEX